WHERE YOUR ACCUSERS?

Live above Your Past and Bin the Condemnation

LS LIFE AND SUCCESS PUBLISHING
www.abookinsideyou.com

WHERE ARE YOUR ACCUSERS?

PRESENTED TO

_____

OCCASION

_____

PRESENTED BY

_____

DATE

_____

Life and Success Media Ltd

e-mail: info@abookinsideyou.com

www.abookinsideyou.com

Cover Design: miadesign.com

ISBN: 978-1-907402-89-0

FOREWORD
BY REV. GEORGE ADEGBOYE

The devil in his onslaught against believers employ his three main powers which are the power to tempt, (Matthew 4: 3; I Thessalonians 3: 5; Mark 1:13; Luke 4:2), the power to deceive by statement, appearance and influence and the power to accuse (Zechariah 3: 1; The Bible says, 'the accuser of our brethren...accuses them before...God, day and night Revelations 12:10. Have you been falsely accused by anyone at anytime for anything? Joseph was wrongly accused of rape and imprisoned. It is something you should expect as a disciple of the Lord. The night before His death people '...tried to find something false against Jesus so they could kill Him' (Matthew 26:59 NCV). Jesus has been there. Satan will never stop trying to engage you in the blame game through your thoughts and emotions. If he can not do it directly he is known to employ the services of other human beings. If you allow Satan a foot hold in this area you will lose! Paul said, 'Do not let yourself be overcome by evil...overcome...evil with good' (Romans 12:21 AMP).

As a believer one of the things you are going to have to do is to decide how much ground you will give to '...the accuser...' It's not God who makes you feel guilty; He wants you to know you're loved and forgiven. That's why Paul writes: '…Who shall come forward and accuse…those whom God has chosen…Christ…is at the right hand of God…pleading… for us' (Romans 8:33-34 AMP). It is not what Satan does to us that matters it is what you and I allow. Stop beating yourself up because of his accusations and by such giving him further grounds. Jesus came to lift you out of the horrible pit of condemnation. He came and by the sacrifice of himself to let you know the penalty for your sin has been removed and its power broken over you. In God's eyes you are loved and accepted and nothing the devil accuses you of can change that. Because of this no one should be allowed to lay anything to your charge.

It's time to speak up, declare thou and boldly too that you will not take all the lies of Satan and his emissaries. "They overcame him by the blood of the Lamb and by the word of their testimony…" (Revelation12:11 NIV. If you keep quiet what he says will sink. If you say something different and contradictory to what he says his words will not stick. It is time to testify to the power of Christ's cleansing blood. Satan is a defeated foe; as a child of God you no longer have to live under the burden of his condemnation or that of anyone who is working for him. Let the redeemed of the Lord say so whom he has redeemed from the hands of the enemy. There is therefore now and ever no condemnation to them who are in Christ Jesus who walk not after the flesh but after the Spirit.

In this book the clarion call is to declare what God has said about you, which you have come to embrace and accept like that Woman did in John 8. The accuser is always present and so must what will free you from his condemnation be on your lips always.

ENDORSEMENTS

When God forgives your sins, He throws them into the deep sea of "Forgiven and Forgotten" with a broad sign instructing "No fishing please."

God never remembers your past sins or mistakes. Unlike mankind, He forgives and forgets! Benedicta Olagunju's book "Where Are Your Accusers?" is filled with divine instructions that will free you from every condemnation your enemies have heaped on you. This treasured woman of God reveals how to forgive yourself when you make mistakes. Through her honest vulnerability she will help you to live beyond the enemies' accusations. Her practical insights will give you a paradigm shift that will usher in that positive change you desire. Do you desire to live a life free of guilt? Do you desire to live above your past mistakes? Do you hope that God's miracles will overwhelm your destiny? Then "Where are your Accusers" is the book for you! I trust the Lord to give the book great wings to soar to the nations of the earth and free those who are prisoners, held in bondage by accusers and their accusations. It is well.

Funke Felix-Adejumo

This book is profound, prophetic, practical and powerful. It is prayerfully written to lift up the outcasts and encourage the accused. The author, Benedicta Olagunju, has positively and scripturally demonstrated that whatever you might have been accused of in the past or are being accused of at present, our God can forgive, heal, acquit and restore you.

Rev. (Dr) Christopher Goodluck

DEDICATION

To you who believe in total victory.
To you who have tasted the bitter pills of defeat.
To you who would rather rise up than stay down.
To you who would never justify your accusers.
To you all, I dedicate this book.

ACKNOWLEDGMENTS

To the husband of my youth, Pastor B.B. Olagunju and our wonderful children – thank you so much for believing in me and for your prayers, patience and understanding. You have always brought joy into my life. I cherish you all.

Special thanks to Fidelis and Olayemi Ukwenu, and to you, Vidal Gabriel for your invaluable input to this book.

To my spiritual fathers, Rev. George Adegboye and Rev. Christopher Goodluck, for your impartations into my life and your unquenchable passions for God, I honour you.

To my dear friend, Rev (Dr) Funke Felix-Adejumo, your enthusiasms have a special place in my heart!

To every member of Focus Centre, thank you all for the love you have always demonstrated and for your prayers.

PREFACE

You may presently be in a situation where you feel tormented by the accusations and judgmental behaviour of people in you life. Your accusers and their accusations seem to have one over you when you consider your present circumstances. It might be that they have displayed self-righteousness towards you because, by your ignorance of how to deal with such people and the accusations they fire your way, you have permitted them to be a snare to you. Accusers only offer a detrimental contribution to your life; and the time to stop the negative effects of their accusations is here and now!

In the case that you may find yourself guilty of an accusation imposed against you, in the sight of Jesus, you are no less valuable; your worth is still beyond measure. He wants you to regain your savour because you are very precious to God, who will rise up to rescue you, in your hour of need. It is God's will that you ignore every steadfast accuser, concentrate on your purpose, and jump into your predestined allotment in life, beginning now.

The instruction of the Lord was upon my spirit, guiding me through the lines of the gospel of John

8:10. My close attention to the Lord's revelation as He unveiled it to me, led to my inspired idea to write WHERE ARE YOUR ACCUSERS?

This book is designed to act as a canon launched against the enemy, who works through those people that readily accuse believers. Their collective mission is to deny your past the right to rest-in-peace, and their ploy is to hinder you from reaching your prophetic destiny.

Also in these pages you will find divinely packed prophetic prayer points that will equip you to successfully emancipate your life from the shackles of both fair and unfair accusations. No one is a V.I.P! We are all equally special in the sight of God. God is our master and His opinion is the final authority, therefore if He has not condemned you (Romans 1:8), then no man is licensed to do so.

I place in your hands uncommon seeds that will equip you to walk in liberty. Sow well to soar high!

CONTENTS

INTRODUCTION

Their voices were deafening and dreadful, well proven were their statements against her. She played into their hands and fell tragically into their deadly trap, now they have got her exactly where they wanted her. Surely, this was the end of the road for her. All the evidence levelled against this woman was undeniable, her guilt was crystal clear. She was faced with instant judgment – but to the shame of her accusers and in her favour – she was brought before the King of kings, the righteous One, the kind, compassionate and impartial Judge of all – Jesus. Mercy attended to her. Blinded by their zeal to finish her off, these scribes and Pharisees made a huge mistake! The Judge's response was a shocker:

"...All right stone her. But let those who have never sinned throw the first stones!" (John 8:7)

Without any tangible ground for argument, the accusers disappeared one after the other. Even the seemingly stubborn ones ended up leaving the scene shamefully. Your encounter with the truth in this book will bring disappointment to your accusers. The torment you see and face today you shall see no more. Isaiah puts it this way:

"Shall the prey be taken from the mighty, or the lawful captives of the just be delivered? For thus says the Lord: even the captives of the mighty will be taken away, and the prey of the terrible will be delivered; for I will contend with him who contends with you, and I will give safety to your children and ease them."
(Isaiah 49:24-25)

The divine hand of the Master boldly writes to humanity:

"Who dares accuse us whom God has chosen for his own? No one—for God himself has given us right standing with himself." (Romans 8:33)

Are you accused, vilified, and shattered into pieces by reason of the tongues of men? This is what the word of God has to say:

"Blotting out the handwriting of ordinances that was against us, which was contrary to us, and took it out of the way, nailing it to his cross; and having spoiled principalities and powers, he

made a shew of them openly, triumphing over them in it. (Colossians 2:13-15)

Whatever it is that you were accused of, in the past or present, I challenge you to take advantage of His divine insurance which covers every aspect of your life. Meaning your sins are blotted out! Take God's word in your mouth and speak confidently to every accuser. Every accusation of barrenness, singleness, joblessness, failure, sickness, poverty, etc. is subject to disappearance at the word of the Lord proceeding from your anointed mouth. Remember the Scripture charges the righteous to be as bold as a lion. discard all your fears, they did not come from God.

The Lord affirms:

"I, the LORD, am your God, who brought you from the land of Egypt so you would no longer be slaves. I have lifted the yoke of slavery from your neck so you can walk free with your heads held high" (Leviticus 26:13, NLT).

The fact that the Son declares that He has set you free means you are free indeed. Peradventure you are being tormented because in truth you were caught in the very act, and you have no way of escape as your accusers surround you on every side, like the prostitute caught in the act. Despite your guilt reassure yourself right now with the certainty of God's word that the lawful captive and the prey of the mighty shall be delivered! His blood has blotted out all your wrongdoings. You are justified! You are released! You are acquitted! Most importantly, you are made righteous. Since He has justified you, He is more than ready to glorify you.

I write, not only to the accused, but also to all accusers. Take advantage of this book and amend your ways, as quickly as possible. You are not permitted to call unholy what God has declared holy, neither are you authorised to condemn any person.

Chapter 1

THE GREAT ERROR

It was business as usual in one of Africa's busiest oil-loading points. A famous Motor Tanker had connected her loading arm to receive petroleum product. Unknown to the jetty authorities, there were clusters of local men in speed boats right at the foot of the loading arm, scrambling for oil with drums and other kinds of vessels. Apparently, there was an unchecked leakage at the jetty that night and a thunderous explosion shattered the peace of the night; a disastrous fire ensued. Men and women were reduced to ashes, the ship, the boats and oil installations all went up in flames. The damage was extensive and to date only the dead can explain the cause.

What is described here is a catastrophe, a horrible tragedy, suffered by many as the result of a harmful leakage being overlooked. This act of negligence constituted a great error, which brought about the death and destruction of innocent people. A great error indeed! Not all errors produce such widespread physical consequences as described in this tragedy; however, when a spiritual error occurs, its consequences can be just as devastating to your spiritual existence.

In a nutshell, being in error is the state of doing something that you're not supposed to do, or failing to do something you know you should do. Errors come in many forms: not just spiritual but also marital, financial, psychological, and otherwise. If you are in error, you are off the trace and completely heading in the wrong direction. This means you are momentarily in a position of disapproval, disadvantage and dislocation. Life may seem complex and complicated while you are in a state of error. This is because you have just deviated off track, and when this happens the consequences can be far reaching and detrimental to you.

For example, the man who is flicking through channels on his television set and comes across pornography and dwells on it is in a state of error. The man who wakes up in the dead of the night and hears the Spirit whisper to him that it is time to pray, yet he turns on his bed and shifts his sleep into second gear is in a state of an error. The man who demands bribes or gives a bribe in order to change and pervert the course of justice is in a state of an error. The one who by any means takes money that does not belong to him is in error. The one who stares at his secretary or

"EXPERIENCE TEACHES SLOWLY, AND AT THE COST OF MISTAKES."
-J.A FROUDE-

colleague longingly for sexual relations whilst married or in a relationship is in error, and so is the one who disregards or takes lightly the Word of God, whether received privately or from his spiritual leaders.

In the bible, David was in a state of error when he failed to lead his army to war and in the process fell into adultery. Moses was in error when he disobeyed the voice of God and struck the rock to produce water for the Israelites in the wilderness when God instructed him to speak to the rock. Esau was in error when he sold his birthright for a plate of porridge, king Solomon was in a state of error when he followed after many women and their gods and forsook His God; and Israel as a nation was in error when they continually grumbled against God in the wilderness. Put differently, *"... any person who knows what is **right** to do but does not do it, to **him it is sin"** (James 4:17)*

Being in a state of error can be tragic not to mention limiting and offensive. You may find yourself dangling somewhere between the 'righteous' and the 'unrighteous', with your very life perhaps hanging in the balance. The truth is that you do not belong anywhere at this point. You do not feel you are as clean as the seemingly 'righteous' folk, yet you are not as terrible, or as bad as the 'unrighteous' ones. In spite of your unannounced, secret self-approval when you compared yourself with the unrighteous sinners, the fact is that at this juncture, you now have the same stigma as they have.

Just like the adulterous woman, caught in the 'very act' of adultery by the Scribes and the Pharisees, whose previous record is not stated in the Bible, your error too might be a dishonourable one. She may not have bargained for the error of adultery in her lifetime, but the situations of life and personal predicament may have lead her into it. Her capacity to resist such a temptation may have been very low, just like your resistance may be low during your time of error. It dawned on the woman, when she was caught in her sin that it was not a mere error, but a very great one! J. A. Froude says "Experience teaches slowly, and at the cost of mistakes." Often our consequences teach us more effectively than the wisdom of God's word and the mistakes of others.

After being apprehended the adulterous woman probably considered swallowing herself up and disappearing from the face of the earth, but this was not an option for her. Alas, it was not just a story, it was a reality, her reality! How did it happen? She probably questioned several times. Could this be a nightmare? But oh the night is still far off and I am wide awake! Was I in my right senses at all? How could I have been so stupid?

> TO BE WRONG IS NOTHING, UNLESS YOU CONTINUE TO REMEMBER IT."
>
> -CONFUCIUS-

When she stopped thinking and looked around, her proficient accusers were geared up, and had closely barricaded her in every direction, and not without their heavy hammers of frustration. They painfully tied up her soft hands, and pulled her heartlessly, with no regard for the uniqueness she represented in God's glory.

Then the Scribes and Pharisees brought to Him a woman caught in adultery. And when they had set her in the midst, they said to Him, Teacher, this woman was caught in adultery, in the very act (John 8:3).

The scenario here may describe you. You might be in a grave situation that even threatens your life. The bottomline is, you slipped terribly, and you messed up to the point that you cannot deny the accusation. You were caught red-handed; you were captured in the 'very act'. Now your back is against the wall. Your accusers waited for so long to nab you in your wrongdoing, and unfortunately, you played into their hands. They rejoiced over you when it happened, and now, your head is shamefully bowed because of your great error! The tormentors of your life may have always felt you did not deserve the favours you have been experiencing both with God and men, now; you may appear to be an evidence of disgrace. You have become their figure of fun. The dream of your persecutors is to put you to shame in the presence of the whole world and they plan to bring you before the judge and have you sentenced for your sin.

There is good news though because, fortunately for you, your case has been referred to the right Judge, the one described as righteous and merciful and if you have a relationship with Him, then He is already standing up to rescue you. Anyone rescued by Him becomes free indeed; He will make your errors things of the past! "To be wrong is nothing," according to Confucius, a Chinese Moralist, "unless you continue to remember it."

The past is past in God's way of working, the bible talks about the blessedness of those whose sins are not remembered, who are made righteous apart from their works (Isaiah 43:25; Roman 4:6). You how live here in the

"One reason God created time was so there would be a place to bury the failures of the past."
-JAMES LONG-

present, and a great and bright future awaits you because he did not deliver you from your past into a bad situation but into a better future. As far as He is concerned, you have not lost your value and He is not condemning you. He is not disappointed at all because He died for this single reason – that you may have life and have it more abundantly.

Perhaps you are in the midst of people who accuse you and vividly recall how you fell from grace during your moment of error, people who have now outlined a path for you, and have taken the job of monitoring any advancement of your life within the "box" or path they have placed you. Every attempt you make to step out past the boundaries of the path they have charted for you will be interpreted as a step of disaster in their eyes.

As helpless as you appear to be today in the hands of

your accusers, be assured that the Helper of the helpless is very much alive. He is divine, He cannot be manipulated and He has an eternal history of proven integrity. The bible puts it this way:

"God is not a man that He should lie. He is not a human, that he should change His mind. Has He ever spoken and failed to act? Has He ever promised and not carried it through?" (Numbers 23:19)

God is in control of everything! The opinion of men will not change His mind concerning you. Even when your accusers appear to be in charge, be persuaded that they are not. God is in charge and He is the LORD of all. He knows exactly the plots going on against you, and He has His own grand design to help you out. Do not allow yesterday's error to use up too much of today. It is said that time "heals every wound." James Long reminds us that "One reason God created time was so there would be a place to bury the failures of the past." Take a break from your worries and prepare to jump out of the trap! Your accusers are history!

This they said, testing Him, that they might have something of which to accuse Him. But Jesus stooped down and wrote on the ground with His finger, as though He did not hear. (John 8:6)

Your case is now before the righteous Judge who is no longer looking at your error, but who rather sees your beautiful future, which He has reserved for you; one that is colourful and bright, and that He fully intends to establish you in! Your job is to partner with Jesus to bring about His ultimate plan for your life.

For I know the thoughts that I think towards you, says the Lord, thoughts of peace and not of evil, to give you a future and a hope. (Jeremiah 29:11)

You are so precious to God that He hates to see you suffer. It does not please Him to see you in pain, be it physical, emotional, financial or any other aspect of your life. Christ came to address all those that have been bringing you pain. He came with a purpose, and that was to destroy the darkness that pervades your life. He came to deliver you from the spirit of infirmity; from cancer, asthma, fibroid, glaucoma, and dermatitis, diseases of the lungs and kidney; from HIV, barrenness, low sperm count, high blood pressure, paralyses, epilepsy; and from your accusers as it is written:

"...For this purpose the Son of God was manifested, that He might destroy the works of the devil."
(I John 3:8)

He has come to deliver you from these powerful forces that rise up against you, so that He may deliver you into the fullness of life for you to abundantly enjoy, He came to set you free, therefore you are free indeed, from the bondage of every form of error and shame, loneliness and rejection, stagnation and hardship.

> "SOMEONE WHO HAS COMMITTED A MISTAKE AND DOES NOT CORRECT IT, IS COMMITTING ANOTHER MISTAKE."
> -CONFUCIUS-

In the words of **Mary Baker Eddy**, *"Disease is an image of thought externalized…We classify disease as error, which nothing but Truth or Mind can heal…Disease is an experience of so-called mortal mind. It is fear made manifest on the body."*

It is not at all pleasant to be in a state of error. And being captured by those who accuse can be even more unpleasant. But if you are now standing before God having repented, He is letting you know that you are a brand new person. He said it in His word:

"If anyone is in Him, he is a new creature. Old things have passed away, and all things are now new." (2 Corinthians 5:17)

Error in your life can become a burdensome weight if

you do not admit it and repent.
Richard Needham has it that
"S*trong people make as many and
as ghastly mistakes as weak people.
The difference is that strong people
admit them and laugh at them. That
is how they become strong."*
*Confucius opines that "someone who has committed a mistake
and does not correct it, is committing another mistake."*

TO BE WRONG IS
NOTHING, UNLESS
YOU CONTINUE TO
REMEMBER IT."
-CONFUCIUS-

A man who refuses to admit his errors and correct
them can never be strong and do exploits, but if he
renounces and forsakes them, he will bounce back and
be strong again. "Someone who has committed a
mistake and does not correct it," Confucius opines, "is
committing another mistake."

As hard as it may be to stand accused, even if the
accusations are valid, realise that your accusers are not
without errors themselves, they may just have been
more successful at hiding theirs than you. Yours have
come to the surface because God wants you rescued
and delivered completely. He wants you released and
absolutely set free.

Nothing could be more devastating than being caught
in the very act of your error. The experience may be a

very disgraceful and embarrassing one for you, but as terrible as it was however, Jesus did not condemn the woman caught in adultery; instead, He dealt with the situation from a different view in order to rescue her. You must come to know unequivocally that when people misunderstand you, Jesus understands you and will stand with you in your time of need; especially when others turn their back on you.

Christ knows your plight and has applied the right remedial methods to rescue you from your accusers. He knows the right questions to ask that will frighten them and scare them away. He knows what to do, and how to do it in order to make sure you are delivered. He may not do it the way you expect, or in the conventional way. His ways are not our ways and His thoughts completely different from the way we think **(Isaiah 55:8)**. Do not be surprised when He chooses to do things completely different from your expectations. All you should look forward to is your eventual way of escape, which He has designed by Himself.

Considering the woman once again, one would have expected at least one righteous person among the accusers that would have been bold enough to cast a stone in judgement. Unfortunately, each of them had their sins living with them daily, but still they enjoyed seeing other people sad, sorrowful and feeling condemned. None of them could say why they would not cast the first stone. The war of the conscience was theirs; the feeling of shame and humiliation was upon these staunch accusers and the divine method used by the Judge, brought them to utmost defeat. They were all shocked at His methods.

> "IF YOU COME TO HIM, HE WILL NOT CAST YOU AWAY"

"Then those who heard it, being convicted by their conscience, went out one by one, beginning with the oldest even to the last…" (John 8:9)

Every one of the woman's accusers felt so condemned that not a single word of defence was heard. There were no interpersonal consultations among them before they vacated the scene. It was an individual decision. each person took one by one. The accusers were shocked as much as they were ashamed! No one dared to stand to receive another word from the Judge.

Their immediate disappearance is proof of God's unequalled ability to address your persecutors, in the most effective way.

Vindication came for the woman at last. When Jesus, the righteous, fair Judge raised Himself up and could not see any more accusers, He reached out to the woman in deep expression of an undeserved love:

"Where are your accusers? Didn't even one of them condemn you?" (John 8:10)

For the first time, after being caught in the very act, the woman could open her mouth to talk. The disappearance of all her accusers' one after the other, and the deep expression of an unfailing love from the Saviour, brought back her confidence and dignity. Even though she was just recovering from the shock, she made an effort to open her mouth to say:

"No one, Lord." (John 8:11)

Falling into an error can lead to feelings of inadequacy and insufficiency. Being caught in the very act is a perfect trigger to bring about an inferiority complex in one's life. Error can be a tragedy but as tragic as it may appear, once you come into God's presence with a repentant heart, His ready hands are available to accept you.

Helmut Thielicke observes that "One who has influence upon the heart of God rules the world." The world may condemn you, but God will commend you. He is forgiving and loving. He wants you desperately because He knows the valuable potential He has hidden in you. He knows that you are a useful

> *❧*
>
> "ONE WHO HAS INFLUENCE UPON THE HEART OF GOD RULES THE WORLD."
> -HELMUT THIELICKE-

instrument for the expansion of His kingdom. He is ready to keep the ninety-nine sheep somewhere safe, while He goes out in search for you alone. He is indeed a keeper. If you come to Him, He will not cast you away.

"Those whom You gave Me I have kept; and none of them is lost except the son of perdition..." (John 17:12b)

Running back to the Master is an indication that you are not the child of perdition but the sheep of God's pasture and God is more than willing to keep you and build you up so that you never go astray again. The evil one meant it for evil, but Jesus will turn it around to be a positive reward for you. How do I know?

"And we know that all things work together for good to those who love God, to those who are the called according to His purpose." (Romans 8:28)

As far as Jesus is concerned, you are already in His purpose because He predestined you to be conformed to His image. You are therefore not a disadvantage or a spare tyre; but you have won! Nothing can disqualify your usefulness unless you allow it, nothing can keep you in bondage unless you allow it. You are of great importance and value in God's plan; no longer allow anyone to condemn you.

"What then shall we say to these things? If God is for us, who can be against us?" (Romans 8:31)

God is very much on your side. He has wiped away all your past errors. No wonder He is saying to you as He affirmed to that woman:

"Neither do I condemn you." (John 8:11b)

As long as you are not condemned by God, no human being can condemn you. The accusers staring and jeering at you are mere men, and not God. Those who rejoice at the down fall of others are evil by nature. When you undergo a flashback or guilty conscience, you must always remember and declare the word of God:

"Who shall bring a charge against God's elect? It is

God who justifies. Who is he who condemns? It is Christ who died, and furthermore is also risen, who is even at the right hand of God, who also makes intercession for us." (Romans 8:33)

Let it be a comfort to you that Christ is interceding on your behalf, and that God is lovingly concerned about you. He cares about you and loves you unconditionally. He longs for you to be joyful in Him. His heart-cry is to see you live well above your past errors and temptations. Jesus wants to be more than the condemnation of the accusers to you. He is putting before you daily, His commendation as He declares:

"For this very purpose I have raised you up, that I may show My power in you, and that My name may be declared in all the earth." (Romans 9:17b)

When no one takes your side, be reassured that God is always on your side!

Suggested Prayers!

- *Look upon me with mercy, oh Lord,
  and forgive me for my faults.*
- *My God, my God, wipe away my guilt
  and smile upon me again.*
- *Deliver me from the wages of my past,
  mighty Redeemer.*
- *Heavenly Father, be my voice when
  no one else will speak for me.*
- *O God! Cause my accusers to withdraw
  in shame and disappointment.*
- *Lord, I ask that you destroy every mischief-maker
  who takes pleasure in destroying my image.*
- *Oh Lord, my Father, remove from the face
  of the earth every power that is after my life.*

Prophetic Declarations!

- *God shall cause my enemies to change their minds about me!*
- *He shall deliver me from the hands of my aggressors, in the name of Jesus!*
- *Jehovah-God shall raise me a defence where everyone else stands against me!*
- *No matter the quality or quantity of my sins, notwithstanding the volume of my accusers,*
- *God shall set me free!*
- *God shall bring to quick judgement everyone that will not leave my past alone!*
- *God shall come to my aid in the nick of time!*
- *The accusers I see today, I shall see them no more!*

Chapter 2

BIN THE CONDEMNATION

The bin was designed as a means to dispose of waste material. You should treat every accusation that comes against you as a material in need of disposal; after all, it is mostly just other people's opinions, and everybody is entitled to their own opinion, but that does mean another persons opinion of you must be accepted as your truth. Consequently, the best way to treat condemnation is to bin it, as a matter of urgency. You do not have any right to stop people from forming their opinions about you; neither do they have any right to dictate how you will react to the expression of their opinions. It is your right however, not to subject yourself to their negative expression, and to reject it.

"WHOEVER ATTEMPTS TO CONDEMN YOU IS EFFECTIVELY CONDEMNING THEIR PURPOSE"
-BENEDICTA OLANGUNJU-

As you hold this book in your hands, I wonder if you

have given your life over to Christ yet. If you have not, I encourage you to do so because only in Him can you live (above accusers and accusations), move and have your being (despite these accusations). Life outside Christ is packaged with crisis and such crisis generally wages war against your destiny and purpose. All you need to do to have Jesus in your life is to have a repentant heart, be very sorry for your sins and the time you had wasted in the past, and that is where the journey begins. Then confess your sins to Him, and ask Him to take absolute control of your life. He came to this world for one purpose – to give you a new life. He accomplished His purpose and expects you to get your own purpose accomplished as well, which is to live for Him. The Bible declares:

"Therefore if any man is in Christ, he is a new creation; old things have passed away; behold, all things have become new" (2 Corinthians 5:17)

Once you have uttered the simple prayer above, old things concerning you are gone; they are treated in God's sight as non-existent. You are now a new creature in Christ and I congratulate and welcome you to the fold where purpose is faced squarely, and where condemnation is a disposable material that you are at liberty to dump. If you had already given your life to

Christ before now, I congratulate you as well. The next step is to become firmly conscious of the Word of God. If you have given Him your life, it means you should trust Him enough to take His words as it is written:

There is therefore now no condemnation to those who are in Christ Jesus, who do not walk according to the flesh, but according to the Spirit, for the law of the Spirit of life in Christ Jesus has made me free from the law of sin and death. (Romans 8:1-2)

Every attempt of the devil and your enemies to condemn you is only to frustrate your God-ordained purpose. Your purpose is unique to you and it so precious and valuable that you must never allow anything to tamper with it. Anything that affects your purpose will impact your life. Whoever attempts to condemn you is effectively condemning your purpose. Thus, when tongues rise up against you, exercise your liberty to reject and dispose of such an offence – bin it. Remember what Jesus told the woman caught in the act of adultery when her enemies brought her to public disgrace:

"Neither do I condemn you, go and sin no more." (John 8:11b)

If the Lord has not condemned you then you are not condemned at all. Every condemnation from any person is only an attempt to make themself appear more righteous than you are. I am not trying to encourage sinfulness in your life and I trust God's Spirit of maturity inside of you to help you to understand me beyond this short explanation, but you must realise that the one who is trying to condemn you, even for your wrong-doing is equally guilty. David was a very righteous man as far as the people around him were concerned. God loved him dearly and he loved the Lord heartily. By God's own admission David was a man after God's own heart. Unfortunately, for a period of time, David strayed off track from his purpose. He decided to stay at home when he was supposed to be at war, fighting in a battle. He made a decision to please himself, and displeased God as a result. God in His wisdom sent to David a well respected prophet to bring him to the point where he became aware of his unrighteousness. God was not pleased in any way that David fell into adultery with Bathsheba and that instead of repenting; David attempted to cover his sin by killing her husband, Uriah, whom he strategically positioned in the fiercest part of the battle, knowing that he would be killed.

"…But the thing that David had done displeased the Lord. Then the Lord sent Nathan to David."
(2 Samuel 11:27c, 12:1)

⚜

To have a clear picture of how those who condemn you are already condemned, and why you must never receive their points of condemnation into your precious heart. Let us consider what happened between Prophet Nathan and King David. Prophet Nathan came to David and explained to him a story which pertained to David's error; it was presented as if it actually happened:

"And he came to him, and said to him, there were two men in one city, one rich and the other poor. The rich man had exceedingly many flocks and herds. But the poor man had nothing except one little ewe lamb which he had bought and nourished, and it grew up together with him, and with his children. It ate of his own food and drank from him own cup and lay in his bosom; and it was like a daughter to him. And a traveller came to the rich

man, who refused to take from his own flock and from his own herd to prepare one for the wayfaring man who had come to him; but he took the poor man's lamb and prepared it for the man who had come to him." (2 Samuel 12:1b)

When David heard this story, believing it were true he immediately condemned the man who took the poor man's lamb. He even spoke out in anger, using the name of the Lord to establish the punishment that the man in question would face. He hated the man immediately, and proclaimed "The man must die." If the man told of in this story had existed, he would surely have felt condemned by the declaration of the King.

"So David's anger was greatly aroused against the man, and he said to Nathan, as the Lord lives, the man who has done this shall surely die. And he shall restore fourfold for the lamb, because he did this thing and because he had no pity."
(2 Samuel 12:5)

Can you imagine the condemned condemning another man? This story of David's encounter with the prophet describes exactly that. David having committed adultery and murder, readily rose up to condemn another man for his wrong-doing. The best advice I would have given to the man if he had actually existed would have been for him to bin the condemnation. What right did King David have to condemn such a man? If the man had truly existed, he might not have lived to witness peace ever again, especially since the king himself had condemned him and declared him to be imprisoned or punitively executed.

Once you mess up or fall into any sin, your first port of call for forgiveness is with the Lord, and not the king. You do not even know if the king who is trying to condemn you is a condemned man himself. Why must you die or be depressed because of somebody's condemnation of your action or mistake?

While King David was busy proclaiming and capitalising on the mistake of the man that he thought had existed and wronged another. Prophet Nathan boldly confronted him with the bitter truth:

"Then Prophet Nathan said to David, you are the man! Thus says the Lord God of Israel: I anointed you king over Israel, and I delivered you from the hand of Saul. I gave you your Master's house and your Master's wives into your keeping, and gave you

the house of Israel and Judah. And if that had been too little, I also would have given you much more! Why have you despised the commandment of the Lord, to do evil in His sight? You have killed Uriah the Hittite with the sword; you have taken his wife to be your wife, and have killed him with the sword of the people of Ammon." (2 Samuel 12:7-9)

Who would have believed that King David had such a huge, poisonous skeleton in his cupboard whilst he had the boldness to condemn the inconsiderate man earlier reported to him? The man Prophet Nathan had described to David only took a lamb; whereas David on the other hand took an innocent man's life after impregnating the man's only precious wife, Bathsheba. Not only did King David condemn the man that killed someone else's animal, he said "The man would die." Imagine! He even swore by the name of the Lord.

"As the Lord lives, the man who has done this shall surely die!" (2 Samuel 12:5b)

What exactly have you done that appears to be unpardonable before people? Whatever it may by, man did not create you, God did and if people choose not to forgive you for the error you committed, just be sure to receive God's forgiveness. As soon as God has forgiven you, be ready to forgive yourself. Though sometimes, accepting the forgiveness of the Lord might be a huge difficulty for some of us. The moment God forgives you, He expects you to move to the next level. Do not park beside your sin and dwell on what you did wrong, life must go on, and destiny must be fulfilled. Neglecting God's forgiveness or failing to embrace it fully and joyfully can actually bring God's wrath upon you without any remedy. This is because to not accept God's forgiveness is to be stubborn against His will for your life.

As bad as the situation was in the life of David, his carelessness, which almost ruined his integrity, did not stop him from asking for forgiveness. As soon as Prophet Nathan gave the last statement from the Lord, David immediately expressed his regret and displayed repentance before the messenger of God. Amazingly, the Lord forgave him instantaneously.

God is merciful and kind. And so should we be towards each other.

"So David said to Nathan, I have sinned against the Lord. And Nathan said to David, the Lord has put away your sin; you shall not die"
(2 Samuel 12:13)

Humanly speaking, one would have expected David to go through some torture before being forgiven by the Lord for such a terrible atrocity. Fortunately for David God dealt mercifully with him. God is not a man. He does not see as man sees neither does He react as man reacts. What bothers God is destiny. He searches through human hearts before dealing with us. Somebody may appear holy, righteous and good to others on the outside, while the inner part of the heart is dark and deadly.

We should not allow the self-righteousness of any person, displaying himself on the shelf to make you feel spiritually insignificant or inferior. After all, you do not see the inward part of their being; only God does. So only He truly knows if a person is in right standing with Him. If God had not decided to take a measure of His discipline upon David, everything concerning his dealings with Uriah would have been swept under the carpet and David would still have appeared as a righteous king, before the people.

Only God knows what Eliab, the first son of Jesse had done at Samuel's arrival to cause God to reject him. God actually considered him, but the state of his heart did not meet up with God's standard for His chosen king. Even Prophet Samuel, as powerful and spiritual as he was, assumed Eliab was the one to be anointed but he was not:

"So it was, when they came, that he looked at Eliab and said, surely the Lord's anointed is before Him! But the Lord said to Samuel. Do not look at his appearance or at his physical stature because I have refused him. For the Lord does not see as man sees, for man looks at the outward appearance, but the Lord looks at the heart." (1 Samuel 16:6-7)

❧

"ONLY SMALL-MINDED PEOPLE GOSSIP ABOUT OTHERS, GREAT-MINDED PEOPLE ARE FULL OF IDEAS"
-ANONYMOUS-

It was this same Eliab that became David's accuser. It would not be too far-fetched to assume that Eliab had a motive, after witnessing his youngest brother become anointed right before his very eyes, and after he himself was bypassed.

"Then Jesse made seven of his sons pass before Samuel. And Samuel said to Jesse, The Lord has not chosen these. And Samuel said to Jesse, Are all the young men here? Then he said, there remains yet the youngest, and there he is keeping the sheep. And Samuel said to Jesse, send and bring him for we will not sit down till he comes here. So he sent and

brought him in. Now he was ruddy, with bright eyes, and good-looking. And the Lord said, Arise, anoint him, for this is the one. Then Samuel took the horn of oil and anointed him in the midst of his brothers..." (1 Samuel 16:10-13a)

""EVEN IF THEY KNOW YOUR PAST, THEY DO NOT HAVE ANY RIGHT TO YOUR PRESENT; NEITHER CAN THEY UNLOCK, STOP OR BLOCK YOUR FUTURE"
-BENEDICTA OLAGUNJU-

When David was eventually sent on divine errand by his father to check on his brothers in the fields, we can understand why Eliab attacked, accused and condemned him:

"....and Eliab's anger was aroused against David, and he said why did you come down here? And with whom have you left those few sheep in the wilderness? I know your pride and the insolence of your heart, for you have come down to see the battle." (1 Samuel 17:28b)

This is a very typical example of accusers. They want you to remain in the wilderness. They do not ever want you to come to the limelight. Any slight breakthrough you receive from the Lord to be brought to the open threatens them, most especially when they know you are anointed. Eliab knew that David was an anointed man, yet he preferred him to waste away in the wilderness. He was not aware that it was part of God's divine plan to keep David in the wilderness for all the necessary training he was going to need for the throne.

Eliab accused David wrongly, but David did the right thing - he rejected and disposed of Eliab's accusation. He binned it and moved on to fulfil destiny. David's response was to give Eliab a correct and appropriate answer in one statement and then proceeded to turn his attention elsewhere.

"And David said, what have I done now? Is there not a cause? Then he turned from him toward another..." (1 Samuel 17:29)

If David had not turned from Eliab, he would have been distracted by the temptation to major in the minor. As far as the destiny of David was concerned, Eliab was a minor. He was not major at all. Where was Eliab, David's accuser when God eventually enthroned him as the king of Israel? Nothing else was written about Eliab after this because he was an accuser; he was only noted as a distraction to David's destiny. If David had taken Eliab's condemnation into his heart, he would not have been able to turn from him so easily.

By turning from Eliab, David was able to find his way to locate the relevant and more important personnel. He moved his way up to where the king was seated. Your seat is not situated with the accusers; leave them to their smallness, "Only small-minded people gossip about others, great-minded people are full of ideas"(Anonymous). It was by moving away from Eliab that David caught the revelation of being able to fight Goliath. By faith, which is the most important currency we must use to make any purchase from God, David was able to fight Goliath, who was a big threat to all the Israelites, including King Saul!

Have you ever asked yourself where was Eliab the accuser, when David eventually killed Goliath whom none of them could face? The question would be asked of you someday: Where Are Your Accusers? However, it will only be asked if you learn to discard the condemnation of your accusers. Even if they know your past, they do not have any right to your present; neither can they unlock, stop or block your future. Bin their opinion! Move on to the palace where you belong and ignore them.

Although no person has the right to condemn you, but it must be re-emphasised that a sinful lifestyle will lead you nowhere except the grave "for the wages of sin is death"(Rom 6:23). It is true that we are in an era of grace, where there is usually no experience of instantaneous judgement as God visited upon Ananias and Sapphira except in rare instances. In spite of this fact, it is folly to continue in sin and expect grace to abound as it is written:

"What shall we say then? Shall we continue in sin, that grace may abound?" (Romans 6:1)

Grace disappears wherever sin lives, there is always a painful pay day if we fail to repent.

I pray that the required understanding and wisdom needed to balance the implementation of the contents of this chapter will become available to all readers in Jesus name. As much as you have been encouraged to bin the condemnation and dispose off every attack that the enemy has pronounced upon your destiny, you must be careful how you handle your destiny. A destiny mishandled could have disastrous consequences.

As strong as Samson was in his days, he did not exhibit much wisdom. He was very strong but very unwise. He mishandled his destiny and paid dearly for it. Despite the fact that he was aware that the Philistines were not only his accusers, but also his attackers, he mingled with them until the last drop of grace upon his life disappeared.

The Philistines were God's enemies because they did not believe in His Sovereignty. They despised God to the point that God used them as examples several times to display His powers. God's way of working is to use the simplest things of this world to confound the wise. He used David to disregard the war experience and professionalism of Goliath. In spite of Goliath's professional armour, which he had mastered from a young age, God employed a basic strategy using an ordinary smooth stone which David catapulted to bring an end to his boasting.

God intended to use Samson in a similar fashion as He used David to defeat and deflate Goliath, an uncircumcised Philistine. Unfortunately for Samson, he was in and out of sin, and mingled freely with his accusers, trusting in his own strength until they got his destiny in the mud. In the end, Samson realised that God had departed from him when he got into the deadly trap of his accusers. He died a very cheap death, not fulfilling his destiny.

"When Delilah saw that he had told her all his heart, she sent and called for the lords of the Philistines, saying, come up once more, for he has told me all his heart. So the lords of the Philistines came up to her and brought the money in their hand. Then she lulled him to sleep on her knees, and called for a man and had him shave off the seven locks of his head. Then she began to torment him, and his strength left him. And she said, the Philistines are upon you, Samson, so he awoke from his sleep, and said, I will go out as before, at other times and shake myself free, but he did not know that the Lord had departed from him."
(Judges 16:18-21)

If your accusers had tried several times before and could not get you because you stayed away from sin, any silly attempt to befriend sin would give them a wide opening and a foothold in your life. Their entrance into your life is almost damage guaranteed if you allow yourself to be careless. Remember that the Philistines had been seeking the smallest opening to get Samson, they tried several times, but they had failed up until that point.

"Now the Philistines went up, encamped in Judah, and deployed themselves against Lehi. And the men

of Judah said, why have you come up against us? So they answered. We have come to arrest Samson, to do to him as he has done to us.' (Judges 15:9)

The Philistines tried such tricks several times, but they could not capture Samson until he carelessly fell into lust with a woman called Delilah. It was only a trap from the devil, and Samson coasted right into it.

"Afterward it happened that he loved a woman in the valley of Sorek, whose name was Delilah." (Judges 16:4)

The accusers in your life are only looking for the slightest opportunity to strike again. This time, if you are careless to give them a chance, they will strike hard and without mercy. They are accusers and their duty is to accuse you. Why must you give them a foothold knowing their evil mission? In spite of Samson's awareness, he gave in shamefully to the detriment of his purpose in life. Delilah was the tiniest hole, and foothold that the accusers of Samson needed to get at him; as it is written *"and whoso breaketh an hedge, a serpent shall bite him" (Eccl 10:8)*. Once Samson broke the hedge (fence) around him, he provided a foothold and it was not long before they were able to enlarge it. It is like opening your door to a thief and then trying to quickly slam the door shut, if the thief is able to put his foot in the doorway before the door fully shuts, this is all he needs to push the door wide open and wreck havoc in your home.

Samson's accusers enlarged the seemingly insignificant foothold they had, to the point that legions of them could come in at the same time and wreck his life. Do not be shocked that the accusers are more than willing to pay any price to get you into their trap again. If you do not dispose of the condemnation and accusations of your accusers, they will strike beyond measure.

"And the lords of the Philistines came up to her and said to her, entice him, and find out where his great strength lies, and by what means we may overpower him, that we may bind him and afflict him, and every one of us will give you eleven pieces of silver."
(Judges 16:5)

Delilah did not have anything at stake. Samson was not very significant to her life, she only just met him and could do without him. Apart from the profit she was going to make from revealing Samson's secret to the Philistines, she was also going to become famous, and her entire family would be treated with dignity so she decided to make a deal with Samson's enemies because she had nothing to loose.

One would have expected a strong man, endowed with so much divine strength like Samson not to have hesitated to ask God for wisdom since he CLEARLY lacked it, but he did not. That which you lack may be what the devil might try to attack you with. If only Samson had asked God for wisdom. The Scriptures declare:

"If any of you lacks wisdom, let him ask of God, who gives to all liberally and without reproach, and it will be given to him." (James 1:5)

Life cannot be lived successfully without wisdom. Whatever you are doing, wherever you live, you need wisdom, wisdom is a universal need, and we all share in that need. Samson did not ask for it, therefore he did not get it. His lack of wisdom was demonstrated in the fact that he was aware that Delilah was trying to sell him into the hands of his accusers and yet he still went ahead to fall asleep on her deadly and deceitful knees.

Samson knew about the condemnation of his accusers, and yet he was careless to protect himself, his gift and his destiny. He held on to a woman who worked with his accusers. In the end, he could not finish his race as expected.

The first thing the accusers are targeting is your confidence. Your vision is the next, and thirdly, they want to disgrace you. Do not live with their accusations, bin it immediately! Samson failed to bin his accuser's condemnation; here's a picture of how he ended his enviable destiny and purpose:

"Then the Philistines took him and put out his eyes, and brought him down to Gaza. They bound him with bronze fetters, and he became a grinder in the prison." (Judges 16:21)

What a disgrace! What a shame! What a pity! The previous judge of Israel, who had judged Israel for twenty years in the days of the Philistines, became a grinder in the prison, all because he refused to bin the Philistines' condemnation and live a sin-free life. The Philistines did not acknowledge Samson as a ruler, they hated him, they accused him several times, they attacked him but he consistently overcame them because he disposed off their opinions, until he gave their condemnation an unnecessary attention – by falling for Delilah.

It is a very painful and costly thing to fall into the hands of the accusers, most especially after escaping their first attack. It becomes almost impossible to get out of their trap the second time, because they had been beaten once and they are now shy more than twice. It becomes a great achievement for them because they believe that "One who laughs last, laughs best." Do not let your accusers laugh last.

"Now the lords of the Philistines gathered together to offer a great sacrifice to Dagon their god, and to rejoice. And they said; our god has delivered into our hands Samson our enemy. When the people saw him, they praised their god, so it happened, when their hearts were merry, that they said, call for Samson that he may perform for us. So they called for Samson from the prison, and he performed for them. And they stationed him between the pillars."
(Judges 16:23 - 24a)

The accusers are not bothered about your destiny, it means nothing to them. As far as they are concerned, after tormenting you with their condemnation and humiliation, they want to stone you to death. In Samson's case, he ended up dying along with his accusers, with God's power upon his life. A mighty judge of Israel, who had judged for twenty years died with sinners disgracefully because he embraced their humiliating signals. Please, do not pity them. Bin their condemnation immediately. Remember what David said:

"Please let us fall into the hands of the Lord, for His mercies are great, but do not let me fall into the hands of men." (1 Kings 24:14b)

Finally, you must remember that as merciful as God is, falling into His hands may sound good, but do not indulge yourself in sinfulness. The measure with which He is a Lamb is the same measure with which He is a Lion. Embrace His merciful nature by disposing the accusations of the accusers into the bin, and moving on with your destiny and purpose.

Simply put: learn to ignore all your accusers because their accusation, condemnation, and humiliation is not divine!

Suggested Prayers

- *Remove from my way, O Lord, every nature that is out to pull me down.*
- *My God, my Father, expose and destroy everyone whose mission is to frustrate my destiny!*
- *Lord, lead me back to my first love with Christ and help me never to walk away from your presence, in Jesus name!*
- *Lord, give the wicked no chance to rejoice over me!*
- *Separate me from the sinful desires of the flesh!*
- *Father, help me always to be at the right place at the right time! Help me to do the right thing at the right time!*
- *I desire and ask for your wisdom to overcome!*

Prophetic Declarations

- *I shall not bow in shame!*
- *My destiny shall never know shame!*
- *I am not what my accusers say I am!*
- *I am the apple of God's eyes!*
- *I am the righteousness of God in Christ Jesus!*
- *Sin shall not have dominion over me!*
- *Every tongue that rises up against me in judgement is condemned!*
- *Those who condemn me today shall commend me tomorrow!*
- *Henceforth, everywhere I go people shall call me beautiful.*
- *My case has changed from terrible to terrific!*

Chapter 3

LIVING ABOVE ACCUSATIONS

Your accusers are your enemies. Therefore, if you are in a position where you are being faced with accusations, you must be convinced that the enemy is at work. The main aim of your accusers is to reduce you to nothing, belittle you, and make you feel worthless. It is an attempt to make you feel inferior and incompetent. Accusers hate you. They are happy when you are sorrowful. Your accusers have maps of different shapes and sizes drawn for you in their minds. They expect you to reduce yourself to the size of their maps and when you attempt to move forward, they will become furious.

Accusers are not interested in your progress and they have no concern or interest in your purpose. The promised success your destiny speaks of causes such people to worry and fret. And they will jeopardise your destiny, however they can. Accusers focus on and can only see what is wrong with you, they are blind to your abilities and divine enablement. They are always looking for your weak points and no matter how tiny your weakness is, they want to help you expand it. They become active in your life just to frustrate and humiliate you. Bear in mind that genuine correction should not be mistaken for accusation. There is a difference. Correction is for your good, but accusation

"CIRCUMSTANCES MAY APPEAR TO WRECK OUR LIVES AND GOD'S PLANS, BUT GOD IS NOT HELPLESS AMONG THE RUINS. OUR BROKEN LIVES ARE NOT LOST OR USELESS. GOD COMES IN AND TAKES THE CALAMITY AND USES IT VICTORIOUSLY, WORKING OUT HIS WONDERFUL PLAN OF LOVE."
-ERIC LIDDELL-

tears you down. Correction is done in love, while accusation is done with destruction at the back of the accuser's mind. Satan, our ultimate accuser is always seeking the negatives about you, and wants to magnify it to the public so as to disgrace you and cause you shame. Whereas, correctors are ever seeking ways of helping you become more positive about your life and destiny. Do not run away from your correctors because you really need them to become all that God wants you to be. They are in your life to guide and guard you along the right path.

Eric Liddell reminds us that, "Circumstances may appear to wreck our lives and God's plans, but God is not helpless among the ruins. Our broken lives are not lost or useless. God comes in and takes the calamity and uses it victoriously, working out his wonderful plan of love."

However, when you are faced with accusers, you need to find a way of staying away from them, if you are not in the position to send them away. Accusers are nothing but wasters of destiny. They are simply the opposite of who you are. If you are a happy or joyful person, they sow seeds of sadness because they do not think you truly deserve to be happy. When they see any excitement and fulfilment in you then this is when they become moody.

Until you learn to live above accusations, you will be stuck at the level man has confined you to. No man, no matter how influential, wealthy or spiritually endowed should confine you to a particular place. Your purpose is designed by God, and He wants you to flourish within it. Do not allow yourself to be drowned in depression and stress by living with the snare of accusations.

Let it be re-emphasised that it is to your detriment to

live with accusation; you must learn to live above accusations. And you do this by dumping them in the bin, instead of accepting and dwelling on them. After spending several years in Laban's house, helping him to become wealthier by reason of professionalism in shepherding, Jacob was accused of theft by Laban's sons who said he had stolen all their father had.

"Now Jacob heard the words of Laban's sons, saying, Jacob has taken away all that is our father's, and from what was our father's he has acquired all this wealth. And Jacob saw the countenance of Laban, and indeed it was not favourable toward him as before." (Genesis 31:1-2)

To suffer a wrong accusation must have been very painful for Jacob; especially as it was very obvious that God prospered Laban beyond measure because of him. Laban himself recognised this earlier on, and mentioned it to Jacob:

"Give me my wives and my children for whom I have served you and let me go; for you know my service which I have done for you. And Laban said to him, please stay, if I have found favour in your eyes, for I have learned by experience that the Lord has blessed me for your sake. Then he said, Name

me your wages, and I will give it. So Jacob said to him, you know how I have served you and how your livestock has been with me. For what you had before I came was little, and it has increased to a great amount, the Lord has blessed you since my coming and now, when shall I also provide for my own house?" (Genesis 30:26-27)

In spite of this knowledge, the sons of Laban still had

"THE ULTIMATE MEASURE OF A MAN IS NOT WHERE HE STANDS IN MOMENTS OF COMFORT AND CONVENIENCE, BUT WHERE HE STANDS AT TIMES OF CHALLENGE AND CONTROVERSY."
-MARTIN LUTHER KING JR-

the effrontery to accuse Jacob falsely. They ignored who their father was before Jacob arrived in their home; and several years later, Laban's sons were accusing Jacob of taking away all that their father had.

As painful and depressing as the accusation was for Jacob, he managed to live above it. He did not take upon himself negative opinion to start feeling miserable and frustrated. Martin Luther King Jr. comments, "The ultimate measure of a man is not where he stands in moments of comfort and convenience, but where he stands at times of challenge and controversy."

Eventually, the Lord spoke to Jacob and he took action irrespective of Laban and his sons' opinion about him:

"Then the Lord said to Jacob, return to the Land of your fathers and to your family, and I will be with you. So Jacob sent and called Rachel and Leah to the field to his flock, and said to them..."
(Genesis 31:3-4)

Jacob made concrete arrangements to move as the Lord had commanded him and wasted no time about it. He decided to live above and beyond wrongful accusations.

"Then Jacob rose and set his sons and his wives on Camels. And he carried away all his livestock and all his possessions which he had gained, his acquired livestock which he had gained in Padan Aram, to go to his father Isaac in the land of Canaan."
(Genesis 31:17)

Jesus Christ is our Lord, Saviour, and role model. He was wrongly accused by men, yet He chose to live above their accusations to accomplish His mission. If you live with accusations, you will be stagnated in your faith journey. If Jesus had taken the accusations into his heart, He would never have gotten the glory He received and as a role model, He gave us enough assurance, and certainty that nothing on earth should bother us to the point

THE DIFFERENCE
BETWEEN ORDINARY
AND EXTRAORDINARY
IS THAT LITTLE EXTRA"
-ZIG ZIGLAR-

of neglecting our purpose. When you live accepting accusations, you are allowing your purpose to suffer. If it suffers, it will affect your end result, so live above it all!

Determine in your spirit to live above the lies of Satan. Let every accusation galvanize your determination. Let it put iron in your spirit, soul and body so that having done all, you will stand. Do more than is required and continue doing it, do not give up. Zig Ziglar quips, "The difference between ordinary and extraordinary is that little extra." Be determined to rise above the schemes of the devil and rise up in the strength of the Holy Ghost. Disallow being weighed down by the strategies of Satan because he knows when to time and title his storms in your life. Look around you and be watchful because Satan's intention is to attack you at your lowest point when you are most vulnerable. Rise up ahead of him and attack! Attack the devil in the name of the Lord. If you need to run, run with intentions that you are running closer to the Lord, because accusations not resisted can eventually lead to compromise, compromise can lead to indulgence and indulgence to defeat. But you will not be defeated in Jesus' name!

"THE GEM CANNOT BE POLISHED WITHOUT FRICTION, NOR MAN PERFECTED WITHOUT TRIALS."
-CHINESE PROVERB-

The majority of people fail in life because of their lack of persistence in living above accusations made against them. Someone once said, "The intensity of pressure does not matter as much as its location. Does it come between you and God or does it press you closer to Him?"

When you are exhausted and worn out by Satan's attacks, you become vulnerable. Use accusations brought against you for purpose only, and that is to push you closer to God. This can happen if you are willing. Consider this Chinese proverb, "the gem cannot be polished without friction, nor man perfected without trials." John 16:33 reminds us, "I have told you all this so that you may have peace in Me. Here on earth you will have many trials and sorrows. But take heart, because I have overcome the world." At times you may be tempted to give up or react negatively. No!

No! Be at peace and be comforted through God's word. Take courage in spite of the many trials you may have, you are not alone. When you are faced with trials and

❧
"THE PAIN YOU CAN FEEL IS THE PAIN YOU CAN HEAL."
-MIKE MURDOCK-

tragedies, it is then that you will discover things about yourself that you never knew existed. No matter what your past is like, your future is worth fighting for and the accuser of the brethren knows this. Oh yes, he does! But he will not succeed over your life in Jesus' name.

Mike Murdock once remarked, "The pain you can feel is the pain you can heal." What are your pains? What sort of pains are you feeling? Is it rejection, hatred, false and wicked accusation, failure, loneliness, lack of peace and so on? Has your image been destroyed beyond repair? Are you moving from one devastating pain to the other? Are you believing God for a business or academic breakthrough? Get up and fight! If you are trusting God for the fruit(s) of the womb, a good partner or a good life with good health, then rise up and get ready to fight! Do you ever have a desire? Certainly, there is a need to fight Satan because you have been called to fight the good fight of faith to which you are called (1 Timothy 6:12). Satan is after those desires. Predicaments never surprise God; it is an opportunity for His glory. Whatever glorifies God will enrage your accuser.

To live above accusations, you must know your God and put your total trust in Him, only then you shall stand strong, in a place where no fire can hurt you. When you are the Lord's and you are strong, the fire of the enemy can only burn off the things that bind you and set you free to fulfil destiny, just as He did for the three Hebrew boys. They declared unto Nebuchadnezzar that the charge against them was not even open to deliberations, and they were not careful to defend themselves in the matter. What this king did not realise was that fire does not hurt fire. Job knew this and of this he wrote:

"When He has tested me, I shall come forth as gold." (Job 23:10)

Was Job not accused, afflicted and tested to the point of death? Did he not come forth? Oh, Job did and God doubly blessed him beyond his wildest imagination, forgetting all the terrible trials he ever had. You too will come forth in Jesus name! The Lord Jesus will use those accusations you are going through to stimulate your strength so you can stand tall and strong in the face of adversity.

"The God of peace will soon crush Satan under your feet." (Romans 16:20)

But how many believers are under the feet of Satan, the accuser of brethren? Their lives are in a terrible state and they do not know their God and the power of His might. They have perpetually remained under the oppression of the devil. However, if you know your God and trust Him, without trembling or fear of any evil accusation against you, no weapon fashioned against you shall prosper. Even if it is formed, it will not work! The Word of God declares:

"There is a river whose streams maketh glad the city of God, the holy place where the Most High dwells. God is in the midst of her, she shall not be moved" (Psalm 46:4-5).

Nothing in God happens by chance or by accident.
"Before I formed you in the womb I knew you; before you were born I sanctified you; I ordained you a prophet to the nations" (Jeremiah 1:5)

No one can define you except God. Do not allow anybody to define you by human parameters, your

꧁ꕥꕥꕥ꧂

"GREAT SPIRITS HAVE ALWAYS ENCOUNTERED VIOLENT
OPPOSITION FROM MEDIOCRE MINDS."
-ALBERT EINSTEIN-

gender, your age or your social status. The real you and
your real identity are not defined by the things you are
identified by. But your real identity is in the mind of
God because you existed in the mind of God before
you existed in your mother's womb. Your life is
concluded, established and settled forever. God has
ordained your life.

"Great spirits have always encountered violent
opposition from mediocre minds." (Albert Einstein).
It is important to have a picture of your future when
violent oppositions and accusations, from ordinary
mediocre minds stand against you.

*"For the joy that was set before Him, He endured
the cross and He despised the shame...."
(Hebrews 12:3)*

Do you have something to look forward to? If not,
pray and ask God to show you and to endow you with
the power of ultimate focus, lest you become a lost
sheep in the wilderness of life. Do not allow the
storms and the afflictions of life to toss you to and fro.
Connect yourself to your destiny and your heritage.

Accusations that come against you in life can affect your destiny. Why was Jesus led to the hall of judgement? Why was He going to face those charges brought against Him? Did He commit any sin or disobey God? No!

"He who knew no sin became sin for us that we might be made the righteousness of God in Him."
(2 Corinthians 5:21)

Therefore, if you want to fulfil your destiny, be ready to bear the pain of accusations, the consequences of being accused and oppositions set against you.

It is reported that: *"One day, Winston Churchill was attending an official ceremony in London. Two men behind him recognised him and began to whisper behind his back. 'They say Churchill's quite senile now,' said the one, 'Yes, they say he's doing England more harm than good,' replied the other. 'They say he should step aside and leave the running of the government to younger, more dynamic people,' continued the first man. Churchill turned and in a loud voice said, 'They also say he's quite deaf.'"* (Andrew Carr).

Others have lived above the accusations that come in life and have gone on to successfully fulfil their destiny. You too can do the same.

Suggested Prayers

- *Help me Lord to become everything you have ordained that I become!*
- *According to your word my Lord, empower your angelic host to preserve me till I fulfil my purpose in this life!*
- *Clean my spiritual ears and eyes, to hear and see, and do all that is in your will for my life!*
- *Take away from my life, O God, every source of pain and regret!*
- *Give me your strength Lord, in every area of my weakness!*
- *I ask for greater grace of the Lord to triumph over every temptation, sin, the flesh and the world.*
- *Father, let me not be put to shame. Let my adversaries never triumph over me.*

In Jesus' name.

Prophetic Declarations

- *I have overcome by the blood of Jesus and by the words of my testimony!*
- *I am more than a conqueror in Christ Jesus!*
- *I decree and declare that I am the Lord's free man/woman.*
- *I proclaim that I am free indeed, because the Son has set me free.*
- *From this day forward, I believe I am no longer living in condemnation.*
- *I prophesy that I am free from obstacles that hinder, barriers that keep me back and limitations that prevent a full expression of my potential.*
- *I praise my heavenly Father who has made me to triumph over all satanic accusation, devices, imaginations and all attacks of the kingdom of darkness.*

Chapter 4

ACCUSED BUT ACQUITTED

It is important to know that you stand acquitted of all accusation! Let me attempt to explain what it means to be discharged and acquitted; it is different from being found "not guilty!" When you are found not guilty, it means you had a case to answer but there was not enough evidence to pronounce you guilty, you could still be found guilty if more evidence is produced by the prosecutor. However, when you are discharged and acquitted after a court case, it means you should never have been charged at all, that the whole thing was a complete mistake and you had no case to answer in the first place. When a person is acquitted, it is like clearing out your previously held record as if you were never charged to court in the first place. This is exactly what Jesus has achieved for us! Go into the field of life free of all accusations and excel by the power in the Word of God. Your accusers and their accusations have been confounded and brought to nothing in Jesus name!

By reason of the painful duty that Jesus Christ

performed on the Cross of Calvary, you are acquitted of all accusations. It does not matter how terrible the act was, even if it was so bad that you were caught in the 'very act', and your accusers are well equipped with facts and figures, if God says you are acquitted, nobody can change that.

You and I may never be able to know what Jabez went through, especially in the hands of his own brothers. They probably hated him, and disliked his bad luck that brought so much pain upon their mother, which may have affected each one of them terribly. They must have accused him of coming to the world with a negative package, making him feel completely out of place, rejected and dejected. He did not have anywhere to turn to for comfort. They made him feel very guilty for an offence he did not even commit.

Come to think of it, none of us dictated the family we wanted to be born into, we did not decide who our parents were going to be. We simply arrived on planet earth and discovered our family placement as divinely allocated from heaven. That was exactly what happened in the case of Jabez, he did not have any knowledge of what brought pain upon his mother, either when she was pregnant with him, or when she was in labour with him. Jabez's mother acted unreasonably. How could she have given him such a name – Jabez – all because she bore him in pain? A pain he was not responsible for, a pain he did not know anything about! He was an innocent baby who was unfortunate to face accusation right from his birth.

The history of his life at birth started with rejection and failure. Short of the fact that they could not kill him, he was never accepted. He was seen as a carrier of evil who caused everybody pain, starting with the mother that determined the temperature of the home. When he laughed as a toddler, they read negative meanings to it. When he cried as a very young boy, they accused him of trying to organise more evil. He grew up with his mind being in bondage.

"...and his mother called his name Jabez saying, because I bore him in pain." (1 Chronicles 4:9b)

Growing up for Jabez could not have been fun at all because he grew up in pain with nobody wanting him around. He grew up being lonely, abandoned and extremely criticised. Jabez was not only rejected by his family, no outsider wanted to be his friend. His life was miserable. The accusations from his family damaged his self-esteem and left him with no self-confidence at all. He could not speak in public because nobody wanted to listen to him. He was not allowed to express himself. He was not free to explore the world around him. He was confined, chained and imprisoned.

Nonetheless, Jabez made use of his loneliness and aloneness; he dragged himself to the divine court, went to the most Righteous Judge and reported his painful experiences to Him. He made God see that life had been most unfair with negative signs written all over his life and that nothing positive was attached to his meaningless life. When he had finished expressing his pains, the greatest Judge decided to surprise Jabez by declaring him "Acquitted!" He was not guilty of any sin, or the accusations forged against him by his own family.

The Re-writer of history made a new thing out of his life. Despite the fact that he was still young, he experienced a life beyond his years as a result of the issues he had to deal with, but when the great Judge intervened, the whole atmosphere changed compulsorily. As at the time that his story was going to be started in the Bible, it was a positive report:

"Now Jabez was more honourable than his brothers..." (1 Chronicles 4:9)

When you are acquitted, there is no guilt or criminal record attached to your name. Acquittal did not just happen automatically for Jabez, he had to take some drastic steps. Things do not just happen; you must give something before you get something. He knew he could not carry on living in such miserable circumstances, he needed a change. He had been confronted with accusations for too long so he took action, and went to the right Court of Appeal and the charge against him by his family was dismissed by the most superior Judge of all.

What Exactly Did Jabez Do That Got Him Discharged And Acquitted?

Firstly, Jabez went to the right place.

You must learn to go to the right place in order to get the right response. If you go to the wrong place for help, you will end up having the wrong response to situations. The wrong response will result in the wrong outcome. Whatever the accusation you are faced with, you must learn to go to the right place to deal with them. Your right place must not exempt God, because He holds the entire universe and everyone dwelling therein together; and that includes all our accusers.

"And Jabez called on the God of Israel saying..."
(1 Chronicles 4:10)

As long as you put God at the centre of the your life and make Him your first port of call like Jabez did, your accusers will end up rejoicing with you compulsorily because of the kind of honour God would bring your way.

Secondly, Jabez knew what he wanted, and he knew how to get it.

Until you know what you want, you will not develop the right strategy to get it. Jabez lived with his accusers who had thrown at him harsh measures of accusations since the time he was born, but eventually his fortune turned around for the better. He discovered that he wanted more from life, carried out enough research and went to the right field to get the right result. He prayed the right prayer and his prayers touched heaven.

"Oh that you would bless me indeed, and enlarge my territory, that your hand would be with me, and that you would keep me from evil, that I may not cause pain!" (1 Chronicles 4:10b)

From the passage above, we are able to see that Jabez

had already researched his assignment very well before submitting it. He did not mess up with his homework at all. As Jabez was about to approach the Lord, he knew that he had a burden for the following:

(i).   A desperate need for blessing
(ii).   A desire for enlargement
(iii).   An aspiration for God's divine touch
(iv).   Divine protection from evil
(v).   To shift from causing pain to bringing pleasure

Jabez went to God with heaviness of heart but strong faith and the Lord in His mercy answered his prayers. The heavens were opened and the storehouse of God's bounty was directed towards Jabez.

"So God granted him what he requested."
(1 Chronicles 4:10d)

The fact that Jabez's request was granted is a sure proof that he was discharged, and acquitted by God. He went to the highest court where the highest authority operates and the result he got was all that he requested for.

Have you been suffering from smallness – seeing things from a narrow or limited perspective? Do you desire an enlargement of your perspective? Are you aspiring for God's divine touch? Is your heart-cry for God to protect you from evil? Have you been the cause of pain everywhere you go and desperately desire that your life would bring pleasure to others?

The only way out of your predicament is to call on Jesus. His main mission is to advocate on your behalf, discharge and get you acquitted. He said it is finished. Everything negative in your life is finished because Jesus declared it so.

Once you have been acquitted, you will definitely become honourable and this place of honour is where your accusers can never get to bring you down or hold you back. They do not belong there. It is a place where somebody that knew your history and where you were in the past at the other side of the pain would see you and ask **"Where Are Your Accusers?"** Pleasurably, you will look round in your place of rest and acquittal and discover that none of your accusers could stick around because of their own guilt and shame. Now that you are acquitted, your accusers will be in the chains of inferiority complex and shame unless they repent, because the Lord has just visited you, and you are prospering..

As a final point for this chapter, if you are the person doing the accusing, packaging accusations of all sizes daily, be warned! The previous shame and disgrace that was once upon your captive is definitely coming upon your head and that of your entire household unless you repent. God is interested in getting you to a place of envy where people would desire to be like you. He can only do that if you choose to stop accusing people. If you are an accuser, you are God's enemy. He does not need any employee to carry out judgement on His behalf. Even if the accused is caught in the 'very act', choose correction in love instead of accusation. The truth of the matter is that there is no glory in the lives of accusers; you will always look miserable and frustrated. Accusers are people who complain wherever they go; they do not have the joy of the Lord in their hearts. No matter what their attire or how much their level of income, they never stand out as being distinguished because something of great importance is missing in their lives – GLORY.

When glory is missing, the grave is open, the grave of sorrow, frustration, lack, and unfulfilment. This fact should encourage you to abstain from accusing people and to find something profitable to do with your precious time? Remember, God is going to ask you about your time when you appear before Him. Let the last accusation you packaged yesterday be the last one you delivered. Any newly-packaged accusations you may have ready for delivery today should be disposed of in the bin! If you throw the accusations away undelivered, great peace of God that passes all human understanding awaits you. God bless you as you change your status from being an accuser to an adviser.

Turning the focus back to the accused, following the triumph of our Saviour's intervention in the life of the woman caught in the very act of adultery; Christ rose from writing His arguments on the sand and said:

"Where are your accusers? Didn't even one of them condemn you?" (John 8:10)

This will henceforth be the testimony of every person reading this right now, the Lord has intervened and His word has been declared, all your accusers will disappear at the sound of His Word. I encourage you to take God's word in your mouth and speak to every accusation of barrenness, every accusation of singleness, every accusation of joblessness, every accusation of sickness, every accusation of poverty in your own life and the life of your family. These accusations have been removed; they cannot stand up against you before God, even if you were guilty as charged, His word says that the lawful captive and the prey of the mighty will be delivered! His blood has blotted out all your wrongdoings for:

"... those whom He thus foreordained, He also called; and those whom He called, He also justified (acquitted, made righteous, putting them into right standing with Himself). And those whom He justified, He also glorified [raising them to a heavenly dignity and condition or state of being]."
(Romans 8:30, Paraphrase)

Suggested Prayers

- *Lord Jesus, set me free from the guilt of my past.*
- *Bring to quick judgement everyone who is using my past against me.*
- *Give me the grace to live above sin.*
- *Lord Jesus, help me to stand firmly in the freedom with which you have made me free*
- *Lord Jesus, free me from all things that can make a person's life miserable - like fear, inferiority complex, unbelief, insecurity, etc.*
- *Confound the accusations of my accusers and deliver me from their hands.*
- *Help me to understand that you have blotted my errors and my sins and have acquitted me of every wrong.*

Prophetic Declarations

- *Just as the three Hebrews boys were loosed and unhurt in the flames of King Nebuchadnezzar, I declare this day that the fire of the enemy shall not hurt me!*
- *Every garment of heaviness, reproach and shame is torn off my life henceforth!*
- *I confess that I am not under any bondage to the enemy in any area of my life.*
- *I decree and declare that I am free from all evil influences and manoeuvrings of wicked and false accusations.*
- *I reject pain! I reject loneliness! I reject failure!*
- *I reject sickness! I reject poverty!*
- *I reject heartbreak, in Jesus mighty name!*
- *I am justified in the name of Jesus and*
- *I have right standing with God*
- *My accusers and their accusation have disappeared, they have become like a non existent thing*

in Jesus name.

Chapter 5

YOU ARE STILL VALUABLE

To help you understand the principle of intrinsic value, here's an experiment that will explain this statement of value to us better than anything else. Have you got any cash in the form of notes as you read this page? If you do, please bring it out and carefully carry out the following instructions:

1).   Squeeze it very tightly into a ball
2).   Rumple it underneath your feet,
       with or without your shoes on
3).   Pick it up and try to straighten it
       with your hand

To go a bit further, do the following:

4).   Throw it inside water, bring it out,
       and wait for it to dry up.
5).   Go an extra mile, try and tear a bit of it,
       or even into two equal parts.

6).   Get an adhesive tape and join the two
equal halves together.

7).   Then, confidently go into a shop, pick
an item from the shelf.

8).   Go to the pay-point and pay with that same
cash-note you have dealt mercilessly with.

To your surprise and amazement, the cashier will gladly or indifferently receive it from you, and you will walk boldly out of the shop without any harassment.

Undoubtedly, this will sound very strange; in particular if it has never occurred to you that a cash-note cannot loose its value no matter what is done to it. With all the negative torture carried out on the currency bill/note, it retains the same value that it had when it was first printed. By the way, so do you!

Have you been battered by all kinds of accusations from left, right and centre? Without question the most painful experiences come from unexpected angles. Have you been tortured, despised, rejected, neglected and abandoned? Are you being haunted by false accusations from people? Even if it was not a false charge against you, and you were actually caught in the very act, you are still valuable.

You are not only valuable to God, but valuable to yourself, and to the people God is sending you to. No matter what you have been through in the past, let it remain in the past. Today is a new day and something good is about to happen to you. No matter how squeezed you are, irrespective of how rumpled you have been in the past, I want to let you know that you are still valuable. In fact your value is great.

Jesus Christ already paid the price for your errors when He died for you on the cross of Calvary. The only price you now need to pay is to accept His love for you. His love is waiting desperately for you and wants to embrace you. He wants to refresh, renew and restore your value. Do not allow the lies of the world to keep you in the dark. You are a child of Light, and your Father dispels all darkness. Stop standing in the dark and stop putting your destiny in a place of reproach. Get yourself into the place of brightness and hope.

One thing you should not allow the enemy to steal from you is your hope. Hope can be very crucial and powerful if channelled correctly. With it, you can overcome any mountain. Your hope should not be placed in any man, because people are mere flesh who can choose to become petty and moody and can easily change their minds about you; singing "Hosanna!" today, "Crucify him!" tomorrow. People are unstable and very inconsistent by virtue of human nature, but you belong to a Father who is stronger than a rock; immovable and steadfast.

Therefore, if you belong to Jesus, you must strive to be like Him. You should work to resemble Him in all aspects of your life as you seek to remain steadfast and unmoved. Whenever the issues of life become threatening and overwhelming, confess your inability, incapability and weakness to Him and exchange it for His strength.

"Deliver me out of the mire, And let me not sink, Let me be delivered from those who hate me, and out of the deep waters. Let not the floodwater overflow me, nor let the deep swallow me up, and let not the pit shut its mouth on me. Hear me Lord, for your loving kindness is good, turn to me according to the multitude of your tender mercies, and do not hide your face from your servant. For I am in trouble; hear me speedily, draw near to my soul, and redeem it; deliver me because of my enemies." (Psalm 69:14-18)

In case your accusation is not false, which mean the

'Scribes' and 'Pharisees' have caught you in the 'very act', you must reassure yourself that you are still valuable; no matter what is happening to you at the moment. This is not the time to neglect God and go seeking after someone to confide in who may not be there tomorrow. You are not even sure if the person you have chosen as your greatest confidant can be trusted. Having many people around you is not as great as having a few right people. When you are not sure of whom your accusers are, it is important to divert all your strength and energy to expressing yourself to the Lord. Confess to Him and let Him see how sorry and repentant you are. He has a way of turning your shame to fame, your trial to triumph, and your tests into testimonies. Do not feel too big or too small to express your heart to God. He is more than able to help you. A small man stands on others but a great man stands on God.

"You know my reproach, my shame, and my dishonour; My adversaries are all before you. Reproach has broken my heart, and I am full of heaviness; I looked for someone to take pity, but there was none, and for comforters, but I found none." (Psalm 69:19-20)

If you come to God humbly and sincerely, He knows how to handle your accusers. Right before them, He will restore you to more than what you were before you fell. Not only will He help you maintain your restored value, He will add more to you in all ramifications. You may appear to be a prisoner today, with the words of your accusers ringing in your ears every now and then; but it is important to dispose of those words because you more valuable to Him and more than the sum total of what other people say you are. You are not their prisoner, you belong to God, and He will bring the best out of you.

"For the Lord hears the poor, and does not despise His prisoners. For God will save Zion and build the cities of Judah, that they may dwell there and possess it." (Psalm 69:33,35)

How To Live With Value
To be able to live successfully, with your value intact irrespective of whatever you have been through in life, prayerfully follow these steps and get ready to see a huge transformation in your orientation:

Step 1: You must be aware of your value.

What is your worth? What has God deposited in you? How does He see you? If you are fortunate enough to become greatly aware of the value God has placed on you, becoming what God has destined you for will not be difficult. No matter what you go through, the consciousness of your value keeps you moving, it helps you to continually advance value-wise. Even when people are not able to read your value at the moment, it is undeniable because it is intrinsic! You must never sell it for anything in the world. There is a huge price tag on you that only those who are aware of your value can get close to touching.

Everything you have been through came to make you strong and powerful. As you become the exact image in God's mind for you, your value increases by the day. Just as you are able to recognise the value of ten pounds or ten dollars when you hold it, you must recognise your own value which is your worth, your purpose and your reason for living in this world. Whatever you went through or you are still going through in life is meant to thoroughly refine you to become all that God wants you to be.

"Behold I have refined you, but not as silver; I have tested you in the furnace of affliction. For My own sake, for My own sake, I will do it; for how should My name be profaned? And I will not give My glory to another." (Isaiah 48:10)

Step 2: You must never exchange your value for anything in the world.

Sometimes, life is not as fair as we expect. "Life will not give you what you desire but what you demand," goes the saying. What has life dished out to you, or what is life giving to you at the moment? Are you tired, hungry or angry? Are you sick, weak and wearied? Are you fainting, falling and feeble? God is aware of everything. No matter what, you must know that you retain your value. Do not bring yourself a temporary solution that could permanently become a thorn in your flesh. Do not use what you are going through at the moment to either exchange or sell your value. Your value is a very crucial thing in your life. It is your birthright. Keep it very well. Guard it jealously!

"Therefore thus says the Lord God of hosts: O My people, who dwell in Zion, do not be afraid of the Assyrian. He shall strike you with a rod and lift up his staff against you, in the manner of Egypt. For

yet a very little while and the indignation will cease, as will My anger in their destruction. And the Lord of hosts will stir up a scourge for him like the slaughter of Midian at the rock of Oreb; as His rod was on the sea, so will He lift it up in the manner of Egypt." (Isaiah 10:24-26)

Every battle you are facing today, in particular the ones coming from your numerous accusers will definitely be in the manner of Egypt. Do not throw your value away based your present challenges. Every time you feel like giving up your value, or you are tempted to exchange or sell it, you must always be conscious of what the Bible declares:

"It shall come to pass in that day that his burden will be taken away from your shoulder, And his yoke from your neck, And the yoke will be destroyed because of the anointing oil." (Isaiah 10:27)

Remember Esau who despised his value and gave it up by trading his birthright for a plate of food; failing to acknowledge the value he had. He exchanged his precious, valuable destiny for a bowl of perishable rubbish. In the end, he wept bitterly but could still not get it back. Somehow, some people may want to argue that what happened to Esau had already been declared before He was born. God is Sovereign and none of us is in the right position to query Him or question His authority. He had declared it quite alright, but if we carefully read and meditate on the passage again, it would become clearer to us that God did not mention anyone's name, He only said:

"And the Lord said to her: Two nations are in your womb, two people shall be separated from your body; one people shall be stronger than the other, and the older shall serve the younger." (Genesis 25:23)

God did not name these two children for Isaac and Rebecca, both of them did as they desired.

"And the first came out red. He was like a hairy garment all over so they called his name Esau. Afterward his brother came out, and his hand took hold of Esau's heel, so his name was called Jacob..." (Genesis 25:25-26)

While their mother was pregnant, God made the declaration, but if Esau had been very conscious of his value and worth, he would never have exchanged it, due to a temporary hunger for food; he despised his value and he lost it completely.

"Now Jacob cooked a stew; and Esau came in from the field and he was weary. And Esau said to Jacob, please feed me with that same red stew for I am weary. Therefore his name was called Edom. But Jacob said, Sell me your birthright as of this day. And Esau said, look I am about to die; so what is this birthright to me? Thus Jacob said, swear to me as of this day, so he swore to him, and sold his birthright to Jacob. And Jacob gave Esau bread and stew of lentils, then he ate and drank, arose, and went his way. Thus Esau despised his birthright."
(Genesis 25:29)

Despising your birthright is one of the greatest mistakes you can make in life, your birthright is part of your value. Without your birthright you cannot be placed, and without your value you cannot be remembered after your departure from this world. Have you ever thought of why people are well remembered for many years after they have gone out of this world? It is for nothing other than their identities which they chose to retain. They resolved in their hearts that no difficulty could make them exchange or sell their birthright and value. They had all kinds of accusers who reproached them and caused

> "WHATEVER YOU ARE, BE A GOOD ONE."
> -ABRAHAM LINCOLN-

them to suffer tough times. Memorable people have had to deal with accusers' attempts to put pressure on them to change their minds about their destinies but they refused. They respected and protected their value in the face of threatening adversities.

If you throw your value away like Esau, you may find yourself seeking it one day with tears without finding it as he did. And that would have been terrible regret. If you disregard your value because of an immediate hunger or anger, you may not even live long enough to regret it because once your value is dead, you are dead also. Abraham Lincoln counsels that, "Whatever you are, be a good one."

Handle your value with dignity by ignoring your accusers because when you reply to them, you are dignifying them, and you are invariably wasting your valuable time and energy. You are so important to God in spite of your past, your errors and the negative reports about you. If you keep your value in effective use for the Lord, you will be amazed, dazed, surprised and shocked at the measure of grace He will shower upon you. Begin to take that bold step from today. Do not ignore the little things that count in life. Value the little things and one day you will pause to be thankful that they were the big things that added more value to you. Remember that you are destined to add value to life.

Henceforth, I challenge you to begin to value yourself even if no one else values you. Regardless of the opinions and conclusions others make about you, believe:

You have worth!
You are redeemed!
You cannot be ignored!
You are very expensive!
You are a crown of glory!
You are a sought after!
You are a voice not an echo!
You are unique and special!
Creation is incomplete without you!
You are precious and honoured in God's sight!
You are a significant being in
God's kingdom on earth!

Suggested Prayers

- *Help me to recognize the value that you have placed over my life.*
- *Father, clothe me with the spirit of excellence in wisdom, knowledge, distinction and understanding in the works of my hands.*
- *Father, I ask for uncommon and unusual promotion, skills and riches.*
- *Father, make me an eternal Excellency and a joy of many generations.*
- *Father, empower me to serve my generation so that my service will count for time and eternity.*
- *Help me to excel in an uncommon field and venture that will attract many people to me for good.*
- *I ask for the unction to do common things uncommonly.*

Prophetic Declarations

- *I am a person of value in Jesus name and the spirit of excellence is at work in me.*
- *No one and nothing shall put me down any longer; I rise above every negative opinion of myself.*
- *I declare that I shall be above only and not beneath, I am the head and not the tail, in Jesus name.*
- *I have received the spirit of power, love and a sound mind from the Most High.*
- *I am fearfully and wonderfully made, the perfect craft of the master craftsman.*
- *I receive beauty for my ashes and a garment of joy and gladness for every coat of despair I had.*
- *Everything that the Lord has done for me is permanent and perfect, nothing can be added to it and nothing taken from it.*

Chapter 6

GO AND SIN NO MORE

Despite the ugliness of error, there is a beauty that comes out of it at the end of the day when it has been properly dealt with. Falling into an error is not a pleasant experience, being caught in the 'very act' makes it unbearably painful but the beautiful aspect of it all comes from what Jesus said as a form of conclusion to the woman:

"...go and sin no more." (John 8:11c)

Error is not a final and total disaster unless you return to it after being discharged! When the Master declared you guiltless and told you to go and sin no more, it was so you could go out and add more attractive colours of righteousness to the world. He didn't deliver you from error into nothingness; He delivered you from error into righteousness! (Colossians 1:13) God is making every effort to see that the dirt of the world is totally erased, that was why He did not condemn you in spite of the great error you fell into. Do not be one of the people that will attempt to discolour the world and frustrate divine effort by going back to sin, once you've been released from it.

The instruction is simple and clear enough: "go and sin no more." Perhaps you were a professional in the error of your sin before you were caught red – handed. You may therefore feel very inadequate to fulfil this instruction. If you fall into this category, there is good news for you. Carefully follow the instructions outlined here and see yourself amazingly transformed from carnality to spirituality.

1. **You must see yourself as dead to sin.**

As much as you have been encouraged to put behind you the picture of accusation that almost ruined your self-confidence, you must never forget the shame you suffered in the hands of those who caught you red-handed and their accusation that nearly cut you into pieces. You must be quick to forget the pain you went through though as it is not for you to keep remembering and rehearsing the scenario without forgiving yourself. You should however use such a memory to help you stay dead to sin, by reminding yourself of the detrimental consequences. Let it spur you to stay in the spirit so that you will never experience condemnation again. It is worth noting that Jesus did not condemn bad people, but He condemned 'stiff-necked' people.

"There is therefore now no condemnation to those who are in Christ Jesus, who do not walk according to the flesh, but according to the spirit."
(Romans 8:1)

If you walk according to the spirit, you will find it very easy to be dead to sin. The best way to be dead to sin is to release yourself absolutely into the hands of Him who is able to keep you from falling and failing. If you depend on your flesh, you will fail inevitably.

"For if you live according to the flesh, you will die, but if by the Spirit you put to death the deeds of the body, you will live." (Romans 8:13)

Sin is only able to conquer you if you live in the flesh. But if you choose to stay in the spirit, sin becomes disgusting to you.

"But if the Spirit of Him who raised Jesus from the dead dwells in you, He who raised Christ from the dead will also give life to your mortal bodies through His Spirit who dwells in you." (Romans 8:11)

2. You must be alive in the spirit, and sensitive at all times.

The need for you to be vigilant and sensitive cannot be over-emphasised. You need to be alive in the spirit before you can be sensitive when the enemy is plotting any evil against you.

"And if Christ is in you, the body is dead because of sin, but the Spirit is life because of righteousness."(Romans 8:10)

> "YOU HAVE NO RIGHT TO ANYTHING YOU HAVE NOT PURSUED. FOR THE PROOF OF DESIRE IS IN THE PURSUIT."
> -MIKE MURDOCK-

Let your spirit be awake even when your body is asleep. The best way to get this done is to keep feeding your spirit with the needed spiritual food. The diet must be balanced for you to be able to go and sin no more. Someone once said, *"if you have the Spirit without the Word, you blow up. If you have the Word without the Spirit, you dry up. If you have both the Word and the Spirit, you grow up."* Just as in the physical you cannot afford to feed on just one diet for a very long time and yet expect a healthy body, so you must be awake in the Spirit. In the physical, we have carbohydrate, protein, vitamins, fats and oil; we also have such in the Spiritual:

I. God's Word (The Spiritual Carbohydrate)

His word is yea and amen! His word serves as a lamp unto our feet, and a light unto our path. Let His word dwell in you richly and keep you far away from sin. His word will give you the needed stability in your daily encounters. The word of God is like a stream of running water that never runs dry, His word is without limit. The Psalmist declares:

"I have set the Lord always before me, because He is at my right hand I shall not be moved." (Psalm 16:8)

The word of God serves as carbohydrate, energising your spirit, giving you strength and stability. His word comes to encourage you when you are weak and it is His word that keeps you going. You cannot afford to stop, you cannot afford to fail, and you cannot afford to miss it or give up. Never give up on the word of God as failure is always waiting on the path of least persistence. Mike Murdock says, "You have no right to anything you have not pursued. For the proof of desire is in the pursuit." In your commitment to God, be steadfast in your pursuit of Him. Let the word of God direct and instruct you in the way you should go.

"It is God who arms me with strength, and makes my way perfect." (Psalm 18:32)

You cannot understand the heartbeat of God if you do not read His word. When you store His word progressively in your heart, you will be amazed at the supernatural strength that will come upon you. I agree with **Barbara Brown Taylor** that *"When the hot Word of God is poured over a cold, cold world, things break, and it is into that brokenness that we are called, into whatever big or small piece we find in front of us, with fire in our bones, to show a frightened world that it is not the heat of the fire that we fear, but the chill that lies ahead if the fire goes out."*

When there is fire in your bones, it galvanises your determination to stand strong in the face of challenges and temptations. The word of God will put thunder in your life and lighten your path in the forest of life.

"For the word of God is living and powerful, and sharper than any two-edged sword, piercing even to the division of soul and spirit, and of joints and marrow, and is a discerner of the thoughts and intents of the heart." (Hebrews 4:12)

II. Prayer (The Spiritual Protein)

Prayer serves as protein; your body needs protein

largely in order to operate properly and healthily. Learning to pray without ceasing is an essential that will enable you to operate properly and stay alive and healthy in the Spirit. Prayer is the key to communing with God. You can not afford to pray casually especially if you have fallen into error or are prone to err.

"SOULS WITHOUT PRAYER ARE LIKE PEOPLE WHOSE BODIES OR LIMBS ARE PARALYSED: THEY POSSESS FEET AND HANDS BUT THEY CANNOT CONTROL THEM."
-TERESA OF AVILA-

You must come to a level with God where you have a regular prayer-life pattern. If you are protein-deficient in the physical, it will reflect easily in your body, your body will malfunction especially as your enzymes and hormones will be lacking and even your brain will be affected. The same goes for prayers, according to Teresa of Avila "Souls without prayer are like people whose bodies or limbs are paralysed: They possess feet and hands but they cannot control them." If your prayer life is suffering neglect, you will not need to confess before people can figure things out. It shows up quicker than anything else.

On a daily basis, you need at least carbohydrate and protein for you to live a healthy lifestyle in the physical sense. The other nutrients are not only necessary, but absolutely compulsory. Apart from a time of fasting, which is for a temporary period of time, carbohydrate and protein comes as the quickest and easiest food to grab. They can sustain you for the rest of the day once you are able to eat some portions. You will find yourself fainting if you go without carbohydrate and protein for sometime. And the Bible says:

"If you faint in the day of adversity, your strength is small." (Proverbs 24:10)

Do not go without prayers and the word. Neglecting either of those two will make you faint, and once you are fainting, you cannot display strength to carry out your assignment. A lack of strength is what makes you vulnerable to the point of falling into sin. A lack of strength is likely to push you into a great error. When you equip yourself with spiritual carbohydrate and protein, you are wise.

"A wise man is strong, yes, a man of knowledge increases strength." (Proverbs 24:5)

Be knowledgeable when it comes to God's word. Be active when it comes to prayers. It is by prayer that God keeps us from falling into diverse errors and temptations. Jesus counsels us thus:

"Pray that you may not enter into temptation."
(Luke 22:40b)

Jesus Christ who is divine and has so much power and spiritual prowess whilst he was in the flesh always prayed to connect with the Father. If He is your role model, then we should follow His footsteps. He would not have been able to conquer the devil, if He was not a man of prayer. He prayed fervently and His prayers brought great result. The devil went to tempt Him, but He was well equipped with the word and His prayer life was not lacking.

"The effective fervent prayer of a righteous man avails much." (James 5:16b)

Prayer is the master key that opens every door, no matter what the door is made of – be it iron, wood or stone – every door responds to prayer. You have not fought wisely until you have prayed. Anything lesser than praying and conquering with the word is only a temporary measure, those challenges are coming up again sooner than you expect. Tie all the loose ends with prayers so that you will truly be able to *'Go and Sin No More!'*

III. Worship (Spiritual Vitamins)

When you are vitamin-deficient in the physical, you will look sickly. It is not just how you look, but how you would feel. You could be anaemic and feel sickly, lethargic and tired much of the time. Vitamins are more effective and without side effects when you take them in a fresh and natural format. It reflects on your body if you have a sufficient supply of vitamins as part of your diet on a regular basis.

The equivalent of vitamins in the spiritual realm is your worship lifestyle. Do you worship God enough? Worshipping God from the bottom of your heart gives you the kind of assurance, joy and excitement that reflects from within; for the entire world to see. It is not just about happiness which is based on what goes on around you. It is wholly based on the substance within. There is no right or wrong way of worshipping. It is measured by God, and it is not as a result of what you display outwardly. He is more concerned about what goes on within you.

Is your worship true, or just a way of impressing people? If you think you can worship God outwardly without having it come from a deeper place within you, you are wasting your time and energy.

"But the hour is coming, and now is, when the true worshippers will worship the Father in Spirit and truth; for the Father is seeking such to worship Him. God is Spirit, and those who worship Him must worship in spirit and truth." (John 4:23-24)

Anything less than worshipping God in spirit and truth, and, in the beauty of His holiness, according to 1 Chronicles 16:29, is not acceptable to God. You must learn to give unto God the glory due His name. By doing so, He will equip you with His grace that will enable you live above sin. The greatest desire of your heart must be how you are going to please God and give Him pleasure. You have been created mainly to give God pleasure. You must live your life up to His expectations. The best way to give God pleasure is to worship Him from the bottom of your heart.

When it comes to worshipping God, you must learn to keep every distraction far away from you. Let Him be the centre of attraction in your life.

To be able to 'Go and Sin No More!' using the grace of worship, you must learn to build an altar for the Lord. Every relevant biblical figure in the scheme of God did not joke with their altar building for the Lord, as we see in the bible. When you build an altar, you are reverencing God, you are worshipping Him, and you are simply letting Him know His position in your life.

To take a look at an extremely blessed family in the bible, let's consider the family of Abraham. They all operated in the covenant that God had with Abraham because Abraham set a good example of true worship.

"Then the Lord appeared to Abram and said, to your descendants I will give this land. And there he built an altar to the Lord who had appeared to him."
(Genesis 12:7)

Isaac also followed after the footsteps of his father, Abraham; he too built an altar to the Lord:

"And the Lord appeared to him the same night and said, I am the God of your father Abraham, do not fear, for I am with you, I will bless you and multiply your descendants for My servant Abraham's sake. So he built an altar there and called on the name of the Lord..." (Genesis 26:24-25a)

It is with good reason that we call on the God of Abraham, Isaac and Jacob today. They all acknowledged God, reverenced Him and worshipped Him. The Lord made their names great as He promised. I am yet to see someone that will pray in the name of the God of Ishmael or Esau! Neither of the two built an altar for the Lord. Jacob however built more than one:

"Then Jacob rose early in the morning, and took the stone that he had put at his head, set it up as a pillar, and poured oil on top of it. And he called the name of that place Bethel; but the name of that city had been Luz previously."(Genesis 28:18)

Apart from that experience, after staying years working for Laban, Jacob's finally set up on his own as God gave him His grace and he built another altar:

"Then Jacob came safely to the city of Shechem, which is in the land of Canaan, when he came from Padan Aram; and he pitched his tent before the city. And he bought the parcel of land, where he hand pitched his tent, from the children of Hamor, Shechem's father, for one hundred pieces of money. Then he erected an altar there and called it El-Elohe Israel." (Genesis 33:18-20)

You need to make up your mind today to build an altar for the Lord. It is an act of worship. As He enables you to build one, you must service it regularly by creating a sacred time where you will be left alone with Him so that He can speak one-on-one with you. Remember how Jesus waited for all the accusers of the adulterous woman to disappear one after the other? He did not say a word to the woman until they slipped away beginning with the oldest. The moment they all vacated the area, leaving Jesus alone with the woman, He then spoke His mind to her. God is waiting for a time where it will be you and Him alone. It can only happen in a sacred place of prayer.

"Then those who heard it, being convicted by their conscience, went out one by one, beginning with the eldest even to the last. And Jesus was left alone, and the woman standing in the midst. When Jesus had raised Himself up and saw no one but the woman, He said to her, woman, where are those accusers of yours? Has no one condemned you? She said, no one, Lord. And Jesus said to her, neither do I condemn you, go and sin no more." (John 8:9-11)

IV. Fellowship of the Saints
(The Spiritual Fats & Oil)

Oil lubricates. It softens, refreshes, moisturises and it brightens as well. It is used to mix diverse foods together to get a better result in cooking. Oil is used on our bodies physically, to keep us maintained, appealing and attractive. Fats and oil is not a nutrient you can do away with for a long time in your diet. If they are that important to your physical body, you can be sure it is even more crucial in the spiritual realm.

What fats and oil represent in our spiritual walk with God is the association we have with other brethren. When you stand alone without God, falling is easy, and error is not far from you. Since you have been discharged from the guilt of sin and released from the pain, you need to make it a point of duty to associate with the right people. Do not think you are sufficient in yourself and do not abandon your brethren. Most of the important challenges we face daily are battles within ourselves and not with the brethren. Do not forsake godly associations. Dwight L, Moody was frank with himself when he said "I have never met someone who has given me as much trouble as myself." Life is a mixture of challenges and struggles, as well as victories and celebrations; the time to stop the blaming game is now. If you would like to know who is behind most of the troubles you are passing through, take a look in the mirror. Your destiny depends on many things, but the most important factor is you. Yet, even with you being the most crucial element to the successful completion of your purpose; it is equally important to bear in mind that a fundamental principle of flourishing is not to forsake the association of the brethren. No man is an island on his own!

"...Not forsaking the assembling of ourselves together, as is the manner of some, but exhorting one another, so much the more as you see the Day approaching." (Hebrews 10:25)

Be very careful not to stay in the midst of rusty people; those who have stagnated and become stale in their spiritual lives. Be very sensitive and sensible with whom you spend your time. If you run with wolves you will learn how to howl. However, if you associate with eagles, you will learn how to soar to great heights. Who you choose to associate with is among the most important decisions you will ever need to make. Have a moment of reflection and consider all the people you associate with. Look at the ones that bring you joy and increase, then compare these with your experience of those that left you with bitter taste in your mouth and hurtful wounds that caused you great pain. You will notice a stark contrast between how these two sets of people impact your life. One for the better and one for worse. One builds you up, while the other tears you down. One empowers you, and the other dis-empowers you. It is to your detriment to allow your craving for certain type of associations and friendships to drag you again into sin and/or pain. Someone once quipped *"if you lie down with the dogs, you shall rise up with fleas."*

You are now a new person. The old things about you have been erased. Everything concerning you is new. Discard the sinful association and always keep it close in mind that Jesus says to "Go and Sin No More!" after saving your from your accusers and sending them away. Stay away from people that will attract you to sin and steal value from your life.

"My son, if sinners entice you, do not consent."
(Proverbs 1:10)

To encourage you to be diligent in the area of your associations; be mindful of this passage of scripture:

"Blessed is the man who walks not in the counsel of the ungodly nor stands in the path of the sinners, nor sits in the seat of the scornful." (Psalm 1:1)

If you can carefully, prayerfully live your life, not walking, not standing and not sitting with sinners, your spiritual life has the potential to soar. You will find it easier to meditate in the law of God, day and night, because it will be a delight to you. Additionally, you will gain from other benefits, as outlined below:

"He shall be like a tree planted by the rivers of water that brings forth its fruit in its season, whose leaf also shall not wither, and whatever he does shall prosper." (Psalm 1:3)

For those who have suffered at the words of accusers; you fell into the trap of sin and was caught in the very act of transgression. You almost died; you were almost stoned to death and burnt alive but Christ systematically rescued you with divine wisdom and insights. Why then would you fall into the same trap again? Beware of accusers who befriend you; when they kiss you, they are only trying to pass deadly poison into your system. So don't be naïve! Only genuine friends in Christ that are tested and trusted, with the Spirit of God in them will correct you and guide you, in truth and in love. There is a saying that, *"Only your real friends will tell you when your face is dirty."* Do not allow unfriendly friends to love you to death with their make-believe attitude.

"Faithful are the wounds of a friend, but the kisses of an enemy are deceitful." (Proverbs 27:6)

You can only effectively 'Go and Sin No More!' if you surround yourself with godly and God-fearing friends, family and associates.

In addition to these scriptures outlined that will direct you to 'Go and Sin No More!' you need something of utmost importance – GRACE. No man or woman can give grace, it comes only from God Himself; He is the grace-giver. He knows we need it, but we must realise how desperate we are to have it. There is nothing we are encountering now that Jesus Christ Himself had not gone through. He is the High Priest and the great Shepherd that understands and feels our weaknesses. Just as we incubated in our mother's womb for nine months, so did He also. He was born in a manger. He grew up like us, and started His ministry at the appointed time. He experienced hunger as we do, He encountered betrayal, accusations and deceit as we all do.

In spite of all the limitations that the circumstances of life attempted to place on Jesus to destroy His testimony, He enjoyed grace and was without sin.

"Seeing then that we have a great High Priest who has passed through the heavens, Jesus the Son of

God, let us hold fast our confession. For we do not have a High Priest who cannot sympathise with our weaknesses, but was in all points tempted as we are, yet without sin." (Hebrew 4:14)

Life is a huge struggle without grace. You need it to excel in all aspects of your life. You cannot do that without it. Your need for grace is higher than your need for water. It helps you to overcome every challenge, to climb every mountain successfully, and to be a shinning example as God intended you to be before creating you. All you need to do to have grace is to ask from the Lord.

"Let us therefore come boldly to the throne of grace that we may obtain mercy and find grace to help in time of need." (Hebrews 4:16)

Grace is what puts you ahead of others. It keeps you above. It is unmerited favour from the Lord. Since you have been favoured to be blessed by God and to have His grace, you just learn to celebrate and appreciate it. You must also put it into use daily to allow you truly to 'Go and Sin No More!' in all ramifications.

In conclusion, it is re-stated here again, at this great juncture, that to 'Go and Sin No More' is not an instruction but a commandment. The importance of any word uttered depends on who says it. If a cleaner in the hospital comes to the bedside of a patient and informs the patient that he would be discharged that day, a wise patient in his right senses would not take such a statement to heart. The statement is fine but yet cannot be taken as fact or truth. However, if the doctor comes to make the same statement, the patient would have no choice but to accept it as the truth.

'Go and sin no more!' is not just an ordinary statement, neither is it a mere fact, but the truth - only the truth that you know can set you free. It is the truth, spoken as a form of commandment by the Master. No other person could have said 'Go and Sin No More' with the same authority despite the fact that you were caught red-handed. The normal thing any person would want to do in a situation like this would be similar to what the Scribes and the Pharisees did to the woman caught in the very act of adultery. They would have stoned her but they simply wanted to use her case as a trap to accuse Jesus of something. Unfortunately for them, and fortunately enough for the woman, Jesus, by divine wisdom asked them the kind of question that none of them could ever answer verbally.

The best answer they gave was to disappear one after the other. Nothing answers a very difficult question better than that.

"This they said, testing Him, that they might have something of which to accuse him." (John 8:6a)

The customary action that could have been taken immediately after catching the woman in the 'very act' would have been to stone her to death. They still had that measure in mind, but due to divine intervention, and grace that spoke for the woman, they brought her case to Jesus, the Righteous Judge. Who can tell how many people had been stoned to death immediately they were caught in the 'very act?'

To confirm that Jesus understood what they had in mind to do, which was the custom in those days, He did not argue with them. By divine leading, He answered them with the most difficult statement ever spoken to every one of them.

"So when they continued asking Him, He raised Himself up and said to them, He who is without sin among you, let him throw a stone at her first."
(John 8:7)

Nobody was bold enough to throw the first stone. They were all guilty of sin. Nobody could condemn her because Jesus commended her as soon as she was brought to Him.

> *Then Jesus stood up again and said to her, "Where are your accusers? Didn't even one of them condemn you?" "No, Lord," she said. And Jesus said, "Neither do I. Go and sin no more." (John 8:10-11)*

Can you just picture how foolish and terrible it would have been if this woman had gone back into adultery? Disaster would have been the mildest word to use in describing what the result would have been. The Scribes and the Pharisees would not have the courtesy of bringing her again to Jesus Christ to judge. It would have been an instant judgement because all of them that accused her and got embarrassed by the divine question would not have hesitated to take revenge.

Any attempt on her part to sin again would have meant her being described as a slave of sin.

> *"Most assuredly, I say to you, whoever commits sin is a slave of sin." (John 8:34)*

In other words, if the Lord has rescued you from the bondage of your accusers, and has put them to public disgrace by elevating you, the wisest decision you can make is to stay righteous. Do not place yourself into slavery as slavery comes with lack of confidence, inferiority complex, and low self-esteem. Nothing puts you in slavery apart from sin.

"And a slave does not abide in the house forever, but a son abides forever." (John 8:35)

You are a child of God, you are no longer a slave, do not allow the devil and his agents to push you cunningly into slavery again. If you do, you may not be the one to live to tell the story. You may not have another chance of coming before the righteous Judge. The Scribes and the Pharisees might decide to do the customary thing before any one rescues you.

"For if we sin wilfully after we have received the knowledge of the truth, there no longer remains a sacrifice for sins, but a certain fearful expectations of judgement, and a fiery indignation which will devour the adversaries." (Hebrews 10:26)

Never forget that there is a Lamb side of God, and there is a Lion aspect of Him. The Lamb side is the gentle nature that made Him to accuse your accusers with a difficult question that none of them could answer. Therefore, He did not allow them to carry out the customary action they would have carried out by the letter of the law of Moses. The most beautiful display of His Lamb nature became obvious when He said to you "Go and sin no more!"

The commandment "Go and sin no more!" is in between His lamb nature and His Lion nature. Your next line of action as described in the scriptures is what explains thoroughly what each nature of God represents:

"Anyone who has rejected Moses' law dies without mercy on the testimony of two or three witnesses. Of how much worse punishment do you suppose, will be thought worthy who has trampled the Son of God underfoot, counted the blood of the covenant by which He was sanctified a common thing, and insulted the Spirit of grace?" (Hebrews 10:28-29)

Choose righteousness above sin. Get yourself permanently sealed upon the lamb side of God's heart. You do not ever want to experience the Lion side of His heart:

"Say to the righteous that it shall be well with them, for they shall eat the fruit of their doings. Woe to the wicked! It shall be ill with him, for the reward of his hands shall be given him." (Isaiah 3:10-11)

A great future lies ahead of you. Go and Sin No More! There are better days ahead. Hear what God has in store for the future ahead of you, why should you throw all of these away by reason of sin?

"And it shall come to pass that he who is left in Zion and remains in Jerusalem will be called holy – everyone who is recorded among the living in Jerusalem. When the Lord has washed away the filth of the daughters of Zion, and purged the blood of Jerusalem from her midst, by the Spirit of Judgement and by the Spirit of burning, then the Lord will create above every dwelling place of Mount Zion, and above her assemblies, a cloud and smoke by day and the shining of flaming fire by night. For over all the glory there will be a covering. And there will be a tabernacle for shade in the daytime from the heat, for a place of refuge, and for a shelter from storm and rain." (Isaiah 4:3-6)

Be reminded that the commandment given by the Righteous Judge that has just rescued you is "Go and sin no more!" He meant every letter in that statement, let your testimony indeed be "I am not going to sin anymore!" Do not give another chance to your accusers to rejoice over you. Let me finally hide something in your lovely heart:

It is a fearful thing to fall into the hands of the living God. (Hebrews 10:31)

Dear friend, only sin can make you fall. Once you sin no more, you will stand forever, amen!

Suggested Prayers

- *Father, revive my prayer altar in Jesus name!*
- *Remove wrong people from my life oh God!*
- *Rekindle in my heart, dear Lord, a burning desire for your word and give me divine insight every time I study your word in Jesus name!*
- *Make me a true worshipper of your name oh God!*
- *Help me to obey your word at all times Lord!*
- *Increase my spiritual sensitivity Lord!*
- *Deliver me oh Lord from the sin that so easily besets me.*

Prophetic Declarations

- *I receive the power to "Go and Sin No More!"*
- *The words of this book shall manifest as blessings in my life!*
- *I live above every entanglement and every cause that will pull me into the same error.*
- *The power of the Most High God is able to keep me from falling.*
- *I have been delivered from my accusers,*
- *I shall not return again into bondage in Jesus name*
- *My God keeps me from falling and will present me before Himself, justified.*
- *I am victorious over sin and temptation, and live above my errors in Jesus name.*

TESTIMONY

I had only been in London for about three weeks and God had shown me tremendous favour by giving me a job with a Para-legal company. My job involved regular travel to attend court hearings all around London and its outskirts.

On a particular morning, precisely on my third day on the job, I had gone out with my "oyster card" to pay for my travels on the London transport network which includes the underground trains known as the tube. (The Oyster card is a prepaid card which is used to pay transport fares in London, you can top it up at anytime or pay for a week's (or month or year's) worth of travel which is loaded onto the card).

I had just arrived at the tube station from where I would walk to the court but as I placed the oyster card on the reader and passed through the barriers, I was stopped by two gentlemen who introduced themselves as the British Transport Police. They asked to see my Oyster card and when I presented it to them, I realised that I was carrying my Husband's Oyster card. The card was registered in his name and had his picture on it, in addition it was a student discount card as my husband was studying for his masters at the time.

The officers told me I was not meant to be in possession of someone else's discount card and that this was an attempt to defraud the government and they would need to ask me a few more questions. I went with them to a stand where one of the officers proceeded to ask about how I came about the card in my possession. I explained that it was my husband's and that I did not realise I had picked his card rather than mine as they were both lying on the table facedown and in plastic wallets. I asked if there was no money in the card, he confirmed there was money in it but it belonged to someone else. I explained I didn't see what the problem was as there was money on the card and my husband would have to use mine since I took his and there is money on both cards. I explained further that I was new in the country and had only just started travelling on the underground and this was my third day on the job. I asked to see the answers he was writing down but he explained that this was not important and that the questions were all routine questions and I would get a warning letter not to make the same mistakes again. He obtained my contact details including my address but refused to give me back the Oyster card and asked me to pay for my other journeys by cash.

About two weeks later, I received a letter in the post

from the courts, it was court summons served by the British Transport Police, it included the statement he had taken from me on the day of the incident and when I looked at the response he had written down against the questions he asked me, they were all completely twisted with statements like I don't care who the owner of the card is, I am the one using it and other lies that indicated I was trying to avoid paying the required fare for my journey. Thankfully, there was a defence statement from where I could state my own side of the story for the benefit of the judge.

For two days I battled with my self trying to decide what was best. The summons gave me an option to pay a £30 fine as well as the fare for that journey (about £33 in total) and that would be the end of that. That option however could leave me with a criminal conviction based on the laws of the United Kingdom. I prayed and asked the Lord for direction on what to do, His word came through to me that I am not a criminal therefore I will not have a criminal conviction on my records, he gave me words to put down on the defence statement form and in addition I opted to appear before the judge and requested that the officer in question make an appearance too. I sent off the form and my husband and I constantly prayed that I would be vindicated and the matter would be withdrawn completely.

About three weeks after sending off the defence forms, I received a letter form the court. It stated that the judge took note of everything I had said about the summons and has ordered that the summons be withdrawn immediately and that I had no case to answer, it stated that the whole fiasco has been tantamount to a waste of public resources and should not have been served in the first place!

My husband and I went on our knees and gave glory the Judge of all who vindicated me and delivered me from the accusations of a law enforcement officer and a criminal record.

For prayers, testimonies and to order more copies of this book, please contact the author at:

Polished Cornerstones
(0) 7951 408581 / (0) 7704 590789

Or Email: waya2008@aol.com

Ingram Content Group UK Ltd.
Milton Keynes UK
UKHW010755280423
420934UK00004B/279